T0121167

Cambridge Elements ≡

Elements in Publishing and Book Culture
edited by
Samantha Rayner
University College London
Leah Tether
University of Bristol

COMMUNICATING THE NEWS IN EARLY MODERN EUROPE

Jenni Hyde
Lancaster University

Joad Raymond

Massimo Rospocher
Italian-German Historical Institute

Yann Ryan
University of Helsinki

Hannu Salmi
University of Turku

Alexandra Schäfer-Griebel
Leipzig University

CAMBRIDGE
UNIVERSITY PRESS

CAMBRIDGE
UNIVERSITY PRESS

Shaftesbury Road, Cambridge CB2 8EA, United Kingdom

One Liberty Plaza, 20th Floor, New York, NY 10006, USA

477 Williamstown Road, Port Melbourne, VIC 3207, Australia

314–321, 3rd Floor, Plot 3, Splendor Forum, Jasola District Centre,
New Delhi – 110025, India

103 Penang Road, #05–06/07, Visioncrest Commercial, Singapore 238467

Cambridge University Press is part of Cambridge University Press & Assessment,
a department of the University of Cambridge.

We share the University's mission to contribute to society through the pursuit of
education, learning and research at the highest international levels of excellence.

www.cambridge.org
Information on this title: www.cambridge.org/9781009384438

DOI: 10.1017/9781009384445

First published 2023

A catalogue record for this publication is available from the British Library

ISBN 978-1-009-38443-8 Paperback
ISSN 2514-8524 (online)
ISSN 2514-8516 (print)

Additional resources for this publication at www.cambridge.org/
communicatingthenews

Communicating the News in Early Modern Europe

Elements in Publishing and Book Culture

DOI: 10.1017/9781009384445

First published online: November 2023

Jenni Hyde

Lancaster University

Joad Raymond

Massimo Rospocher

Italian-German Historical Institute

Yann Ryan

University of Helsinki

Hannu Salmi

University of Turku

Alexandra Schäfer-Griebel

Leipzig University

Author for correspondence: Yann Ryan, yann.ryan@gmail.com

ABSTRACT: This history of early modern news focuses on news itself rather than specific material forms. Centring on movement through different media, times, and places, it makes the case for a truly comparative, pan-European history of news. After the Introduction, the second section, 'News Moves', explores how we think about and research news culture and news communication, demonstrating that movement is more important than static forms. The third section, 'News Sings', focuses on news ballads, comparing actors, publics, music, and soundscapes of ballad singing in several European cities, highlighting the central role of immaterial elements, such as sound, music, and voice. The fourth section, 'News Counts', argues that seeing news the way a machine might read it – through its metadata – is one way of moving beyond form, allowing us to find surprising commonalities in news cultures which differ greatly in both time and place.

KEYWORDS: news communication, news ballads, early modern news, digital humanities

ISBNs: 9781009384438 (PB), 9781009384445 (OC)

ISSNs: 2514-8524 (online), 2514-8516 (print)

Contents

Additional resources for this publication at
www.cambridge.org/communicatingthenews

1 Introduction

When King Henry III of France was murdered in 1589, France was flooded with news publications. Everyone wanted to know how the murderer had committed this atrocity and how they were to be punished by the crown. Among the many printed news publications was an engraving *Figure de l'admirable & diuine resolution de F. Iacques Clement* showing several scenes, among them the quartering of Jacques Clément. This part of the engraving or figurative invention was soon enough taken up in the pamphlet *Le Martyre de Frere Iacqves Clement*. This image news-element crossed not only media boundaries but also regions within Europe. A short time later, it was adopted in a Cologne workshop in the single-sheet print *König Heinrich der dritt des namen*, which placed it alongside three other pictures of different provenance.[1]

News moves. It is restless. It moves by a plenitude of means, through a variety of media. It moves through voices and hands and eyes, and these means interact in a complex array of ways, so multifarious that it would be impossible to describe them all in human terms. Communicating news is one of the most human activities. It shapes where we are and where we think we stand, it binds us to other people. But one way of thinking about this mass of human interaction – an additional perspective to thinking about individual stories and personal communication – is to move beyond individuals and particular actions and instead think about networks and communities.

The commonality of news, or of certain kinds of news, formed communities (a word derived from the Latin *communitas*, via the Anglo-Norman and Middle French *communité*, signifying both joint ownership and people having a common identity).[2] From the perspective of the twenty-first century (and reading the *Oxford English Dictionary*), we assume that those shared identities are ethnic or national, but in early modern Europe,

---

[1] *Figure de l'admirable & diuine resolution de F. Iacques Clement* (Paris: Roland Guérard / Nicolas Prévost, 1589); *Le Martyre de Frere Iacqves Clement* (Paris: Robert Le Fizelier, 1589); *König Heinrich der dritt des namen* (Cologne: workshop of Franz Hogenberg, 1589) (cf. Figure 3).

[2] 'community, *n.*' *OED Online*, Oxford University Press, June 2020, www.oed .com/view/Entry/37337 (15 July 2020); Raymond Williams, *Keywords* (1976; London: Fontana, 1983), 75–6.

ethnicity was a less rigid model for identity, and nations often had blurred boundaries and overlapping political structures. News and the communities it formed were highly international. Moreover, news publications, both those that were printed and those written by hand, seldom focused on a nation's or region's news. National newspapers came later – towards the end of the story in hand here. So, from the perspective of the time, an *international community* was far from counterintuitive.

Thus, it seems natural to talk about news in 'trans' contexts, whether transregional or transnational. Europe is the framework or point of reference chosen here for a 'trans' approach. Europe serves both as a pre-set geographical and cultural framework and as a concept which needs to be captured and spelled out in its concrete form by the contributions. Despite language barriers, news was read in neighbouring countries, the news market of one country reacted to and sometimes depended on the news market of another country, and postal systems were interdependent and built a network throughout Europe. One has to be aware that the concept of Europe, though useful, is not unproblematic. 'Ever since its inception, "Europe" has always represented more of an imagined than a clearly definable quantity.'[3] And one should be aware: when talking about Europe, one might provoke images of a centre and a periphery, of certain commonalities suppressing others. We might get quite a different picture of hubs in news networks and of centrality when looking at Sweden, for example, in the framework of the Baltic states or at Madrid in the framework of the Spanish-speaking world, including the colonies. Those examples show already that there are alternative concepts for transregions to the concept 'Europe', which is true already for the sixteenth century and not only when debates on internationalisation and globalisation started.

One transnational community at this time was associated with humanist scholars, who formed what has been called a 'Republic of Letters' or *republica litteraria*. This was an imagined community of learned individuals

---

[3] Wolfgang Schmale, 'Europe as a Cultural Reference and Value System,' in European History Online (EGO), published by the Institute of European History (IEG), Mainz 3 December 2010. https://www.ieg-ego.eu/schmalew-2010-en. (24 February 2023).

who shared their learning: sending each other personal letters, scholarly references, manuscripts, dedications and prefaces, and published books. Much is known about this community, individually and collectively, because of the value placed by later scholars on their learning, and the role they played in the literary, artistic, and political culture of the late Renaissance means that their lives and letters have been prized, edited, and studied. Their network has been reassembled.[4] The international communication of news in many ways resembled this network because it was also based on written and printed documents, in many languages, moving around Europe between cities and towns by carrier and post. But it was also significantly different: *newsletters* and *avvisi* were mostly anonymous. They had no intrinsic value as *ego* documents. They were generally not addressed to individuals, and those that were contained paragraphs that were copied from impersonal sources. Most were not individual letters but were made in small editions of multiple copies, often with small variations, and their content was impersonal, designed to be reproduced (although it is also the case that some scholars had an eye on printed letter collections and posterity and so anticipated reproduction). Newsletters and *avvisi* were not intrinsically valued, and so on those occasions when they were preserved this was for reasons other than the identity of the sender or recipient, and they were kept as a series or saved because they were associated with other documents (such as *relazioni* in the *archivo di stato* in Venice).

So it makes a great deal of sense to consider the movement of news independently of the people who wrote, moved, and received it. We can scale up from the individual who handles a gazette or *avviso* to various communities and to the whole news-sharing network that facilitates those communities. However, we must be cautious about this idea of the 'whole'. Even if we were to recover every single piece of evidence about the communication of news in every major research library and analyse their movement through the metadata, we would still be left with various problems. First, the evidence that survives is selective: it is preserved for particular reasons and

---

[4] Howard Hotson and Thomas Wallnig, eds., *Reassembling the Republic of Letters in the Digital Age: Standards, Systems, Scholarship* (Göttingen: Göttingen University Press, 2019).

cannot be presumed to be representative. Second, the 'whole' changes over time. The contours and flows of news were different in 1500 and in 1600 and in 1700, and a synoptic view would be misleading – it would represent something that never actually existed. Third, the satellite's view, showing everything, would also be misleading – because the way in which the network was experienced by those involved in it depended on where they were. The movement of news into and out of London and the series of cities which the news passed through in order to arrive in London need to be analysed from the perspective of London. This may sound tautological, but it is not. In the seventeenth century, news coming to London *preferred* certain routes: news from the German states and the Netherlands was relayed from Amsterdam, and news from southern Europe through Paris (departing on the final stages of its voyage through the packet boats at Antwerp and Calais), as will be outlined in section 2.2. However, news to Paris from northern Europe was likely to prefer a route via Antwerp. To understand the whole, we need to see all of these together, but in order to understand a city's news market, we need to separate the flows that connect, directly and indirectly, to that city from flows that are less influential. The significance of this will become more evident as this section progresses.

This book builds on the new directions towards which news has been moving, which might be summed up in four points. The first point is increased attention to internationalism (not just comparative studies between countries but a joined-up understanding of international news). This is evident in the increasing volume of research which emphasises international connections and flows of news or shows how news should be considered a single connected and interrelated system, albeit one with multiple perspectives.[5] This approach to

[5] Some notable examples of this approach include Helmer Helmers, 'A New Golden Age for Newspaper Research,' *Early Modern Low Countries* 2, no. 1 (2018): 1–6, https://doi.org/10.18352/emlc.58; Paul Arblaster, 'Posts, Newsletters, Newspapers: England in a European System of Communications,' *Media History* 11, no. 1–2 (2005): 21–36, https://doi.org/10.1080/1368880052000342398; Paul Arblaster, *From Ghent to Aix: How They Brought the News in the Habsburg Netherlands, 1550–1700* (Leiden: Brill, 2014); Jan Hillgärtner, 'The King Is Dead: German Broadsheets Printed on the Death of Gustavus Adolphus and Charles I,'

news opens up questions of borders, centres, and peripheries, forcing us to consider these concepts as functions of communication, not geography. The second point is a new interest in bibliographical research and bibliographical sensitivity to form. This focus on international news is made possible by better and more thorough sources and metadata standards. As ephemeral objects, news in its various forms has traditionally been shown less attention by bibliographers in comparison with others who work on the history of the book. An exciting development in news scholarship is a revival of the interest in bibliographic research, particularly focusing on form, such as in the work on ballads by Jenni Hyde and Una McIlvenna, but also the opportunities and value of original bibliographic research.[6] This 'bibliographic turn' is made possible in no small part by funding for digitisation projects as well as online finding-aids and catalogues such as the English Short Title Catalogue (ESTC) and Universal Short Title Catalogue (USTC). The third point is interest in 'big data' and computational methods. News research has benefited from new technological advances, from increased data availability and digitisation, techniques which can better 'read' early modern printed texts, to the advanced analysis of language made possible by deep learning and neural networks.[7]

in *Broadsheets*, ed. Andrew Pettegree (Leiden: Brill, 2017), 295–315, https://doi .org/10.1163/9789004340312_013; Jan Hillgärtner, 'Netherlandish Reports in German Newspapers, 1605–1650,' *Early Modern Low Countries* 2, no. 1 (2018): 68–87, https://doi.org/10.18352/emlc.62; Joad Raymond and Noah Moxham, 'Introduction,' in *News Networks in Early Modern Europe*, ed. Joad Raymond and Noah Moxham (Leiden: Brill, 2016), 1–18; Alexandra Schäfer-Griebel, *Die Medialität der Französischen Religionskriege. Frankreich und das Heilige Römische Reich 1589* (Stuttgart: Steiner, 2018); Cornel Zwierlein, *Discorso und Lex Dei: die Entstehung neuer Denkrahmen im 16. Jahrhundert und die Wahrnehmung der französischen Religionskriege in Italien und Deutschland* (Göttingen: Vandenhoeck & Ruprecht, 2006).

6   For example, Jan-Friedrich Missfelder, 'The Local and the Vocal: Tracing Vocality in Early 18th Century Print Media,' *Cheiron* 6, no. 2 (2022): 30–49.

7   See the projects at Digital Historical Research Unit | DH Lab at the Leibniz Institute of European History (IEG); www.ieg-mainz.de/en/research/ digital_historical_research/dh-lab (27 February 2023). For example, Jaap Geraerts's project on *'Staatskatholieken en Roomskatholieken': The Catholic Laity*

The fourth point is attention to sociology and social frameworks of news, including reading practices and the post, as exemplified by the research of scholars such as Helmer Helmers on the news culture of the Dutch Republic. These developments are interrelated: if news is to be considered international, then it is also a large and complex system which differs in language, form, and social conventions and which needs new bibliographies, techniques, and frameworks to be fully understood.

With these developments in mind, this book argues for a new perspective on the history of news – one which is transnational, takes into account but also cuts across individual news forms, place, movement, and flows, and utilises data which digitisation and new methods have enabled. In this history, we suggest, the act of communication, rather than the study of any single news form or national history, should be centred. The project grew out of Jeroen Salman's 'European Dimensions of Popular Print Culture (EDPOP)' research network funded by the Dutch research council (NWO).[8] The network hosted workshops themed around different popular print genres as diverse as medical literature, children's literature, and song. Each workshop brought together six scholars to discuss the similarities and differences in the way their genre was produced and disseminated across Europe. The participants were encouraged to develop research methodologies that might help to break down the barriers between national histories. The project culminated in a conference, held at the University of Utrecht in 2018, which brought together researchers from different European countries and research areas

and the Schism in the Catholic Church in the Dutch Republic, 1650–ca.1750, which uses data-mining and network analysis and creates a relational database with diverse serial sources. Various publications by Markus Müller, for example, 'Episode II: Let Python Speak to Transkribus,' in Digital Humanities Lab, 23 July 2021, URL: https://dhlab.hypotheses.org/2114, code: https://github .com/gedoensmanagement/transkribus_rest_api_client; 'Episode VI: Finding Text Re-Use,' in Digital Humanities Lab, 17 December 2021, URL: https:// dhlab.hypotheses.org/2322, code: https://github.com/gedoensmanagement/ finding_similarities (27 February 2023).

[8] See https://edpop.wp.hum.uu.nl.

to create truly comparative approaches to various genres of ephemeral literature.

We have divided this book into three sections. The first, 'News Moves', argues that news should be seen as a mobile thing, something that is fundamentally fungible. It focuses on the movement of small units of news and, through this, outlines the connectedness of different regions in Europe. It seeks to show how news was not bound to one news form but moved between media and news forms. The second section, 'News Sings', focuses on an often overlooked, multi-modal source: the news ballad. Focusing on Italy and England, the section is grounded in the belief that these songs were intended to be performed and therefore compares the people and places associated with singing news ballads, finding some surprising similarities. Because music is central to understanding these songs, we not only provide illustrative scores but also include new recordings of some of the featured songs. Moreover, the section highlights the ways in which itinerant ballad-sellers harnessed the social spaces that were already associated with authority in order to enhance the credibility of their songs, a technique that physically reiterated truth claims made in titles across the continent. The third section, 'News Counts', focuses on the opportunities – and pitfalls – afforded by the abundance of news data and advanced computational methods which have become available in recent years. It argues that seeing news the way a machine might read it – through its metadata – is another way of moving beyond form, allowing us to find surprising commonalities in news cultures which differ greatly in both time and place.

Through these perspectives, the book examines the spaces between form and content, between particular stories and news genres, and between local and transnational histories. It looks at where news originated and the common routes by which it moved. It aims to uncover the connections between people physically separated by seas, rivers, and mountains and divided by language, politics, and religion, who nonetheless shared the news that shaped their views of the world.

2 News Moves

2.1 Introduction

If we want to understand how news[9] work, we should think of them as mobile and intrinsically fungible. Studies of news have tended to concentrate on stable and inflexible categories such as the particular forms and genres through which news was communicated. Even studies of particular news forms as parts of a multi-media news sphere have tended to lose sight of the intermediality between news forms.[10] Neither the connectivity of news forms nor the elasticity of news moving between those forms has been studied systematically. Most research examining the mobility of news has concentrated on the circulation of news publications as a whole or on particular news stories. The movement of visual and textual news-elements (a phrase we mean to refer to the small parts of a written or printed news publication that are taken up and re-used in other media), such as news items, excerpts of texts, individual images or parts of images, and fragments and smaller units – such as paragraphs – has hardly been traced. If we follow those traces, we can establish how closely the news markets in different European regions were connected.

Recent research has proposed alternative perspectives and methods, ones that challenge traditional approaches to particular forms and genres and instead help us grasp how news moves and changes as it moves. Thus, we might conceive tracing the movement of paragraphs, not only geographically but also between voices, writing, and various kinds of print; and we can study 'media recycling', the re-use of pieces of news, fragments of stories or texts, often crossing the boundaries between media.[11]

Our first aim is to outline the connectedness and connectiveness of different regions in Europe and their news markets. News cultures were

---

[9] Treated as both grammatically singular and plural.

[10] An exceptional case is Daniel Bellingradt and Massimo Rospocher, eds., 'The Intermediality of Early Modern Communication,' special issue, *Cheiron* 2 (2021): 5–29.

[11] Will Slauter, 'Le paragraphe mobile: circulation et transformation des informations dans le monde atlantique du 18e siècle,' and 'The Paragraph as

shared, and this created, if only temporarily, a mutual public sphere. Our focus resists the drift towards national approaches, which have often made the history of news an instrument of nationalist historiography. This section discusses examples of the mobility of news in the Holy Roman Empire and France, the Iberian Peninsula, Italy, Britain, and the Netherlands. News 'moved' in Europe between different regions with different languages, different news markets, and different publication contexts as well as different political institutions, different confessions, and different practices or ways of handling news. A region in which news from another region were taken up, re-used, and adopted may have had a distinct news market when it came to legal restrictions, a preferred language, political authorities, and so on, but there was an intense exchange between those neighbouring regions.[12] This can establish a partly shared news culture. If we do not concentrate on the circulation of particular publications – if the newspaper or a specific news publication is not our unit – but instead examine the movement of visual and textual news-elements and small units (such as paragraphs) between regions, the connectiveness of different regions in Europe becomes even more apparent. There is no direct correlation between news forms and the later nation-state, and with printed forms (less so for written) it is cities, not kingdoms or countries, that dominate geography.

Our second aim is to sketch the mobility of news regarding news forms. Circulating news were not bound to one news form but moved between

Information Technology: How News Travelled in the Eighteenth-Century Atlantic World,' *Annales: Histoire, Sciences Sociales* 67, no. 2 (2012): 253–78, 363–89; Joad Raymond and Noah Moxham, eds., *News Networks in Early Modern Europe* (Leiden: Brill, 2016); Joad Raymond, *The News in Europe* (London: Allen Lane, forthcoming); Daniel Bellingradt, 'Annäherungen an eine Kommunikationsgeschichte der Frühen Neuzeit,' *Jahrbuch für Kommunikationsgeschichte* 20 (2018): 16–21.

[12] On news of a relatively minor skirmish travelling far through several regions and changing in this process, compare Filippo De Vivo, 'Microhistories of Long-Distance Information: Space, Movement and Agency in the Early Modern News,' *Past & Present* 242, Suppl. 14 (2019): 179–214, https://academic.oup .com/past/article/242/Supplement_14/179/5637705 (24 February 2023).

speech, writing, and print, from *avvisi* to pamphlets to conversations and so on. Small units, whether texts or images, or visual and textual news-elements were re-used and combined across media boundaries. A portrait, for example, first appearing as a single-sheet print could reappear in several single-sheet prints, broadsheets, on the title page of a pamphlet, or as a figure embedded in a pamphlet before making its way into a collection or scrapbook like the well-known one of Pierre de L'Estoile.[13] Early modern readers and writers of news brought together different media in their daily practice of producing, disseminating, and reading news; they never assumed that news was written to be complete or comprehensive.[14] While media performed subtly different roles, they engaged overlapping but partly distinct audiences; and when they addressed the same audience, they were as likely to be complementary as competitive. News forms were designed and evolved with co-dependency in mind. The focus on the mobility of visual and textual news-elements of early modern news allows us to sidestep the risk of over-emphasising news forms: instead, we argue that such forms must be considered in the context of the very networks, structures, and practices that gave them coherence.

2.2 Mobility of Printed News

In northern and western Europe from the fourteenth century onwards, there developed a dynamic economy of news: news covered similar topics, was shared through similar media, and circulated in similar ways, and much of it

---

[13] On L'Estoile's practise of collecting and creating a scrapbook, compare the subchapter 'Reception and Reuse' in Alexandra Schäfer-Griebel, 'Writing an Integrated History of Mediated Communication for the "Period of the League". Or: How Henry III and Royal Camp Initiated and Disseminated News Publications in 1589,' *Cheiron* 2 (2021): 50–68, here 62–5.

[14] For a case study on handling different news forms, compare Alexandra Schäfer-Griebel, 'Acquisition and Handling of News on the French Wars of Religion in Cologne: The Case of Hermann Weinsberg, with Particular Focus on the Engravings by Franz Hogenberg,' in *News Networks in Early Modern Europe*, ed. Joad Raymond and Noah Moxham (Leiden: Brill, 2016), 695–715.

was the same news, translated and cut and pasted.[15] For a taxonomy of the forms of news media that spans western Europe, see an online supplement for this section.

News was mobile in multiple ways. First, printed and manuscript news were read outside the geographical area associated with the language in which they appeared. In other words, people read news in their second or third languages. *Mercurius Politicus*, a London newsbook from the 1650s, was widely read overseas.[16] In rural Sweden in 1653, an English diplomat and a Swedish official discussed the contents of Dutch gazettes.[17] The Swedish chancellor, Axel Oxenstierna, received the Amsterdam papers, as did Jean-Baptiste Colbert, Louis XIV's minister of finance; it was a standard practice of national and civic governments; and ordinary readers bought and borrowed them, too.[18]

Not only news and news media but news printers were mobile, carrying specialist knowledge between regions.[19] Itinerant distribution methods also played a role in news communication. The language used to describe news forms is also mobile; this is symptomatic of news culture and has significant

---

[15] Raymond and Moxham, *News Networks, passim*; Raymond, *The News in Europe*.

[16] Joad Raymond, 'International News and the Seventeenth-Century English Newspaper,' in *Not Dead Things: The Dissemination of Popular Print in Britain, Italy, and the Low Countries, 1500–1900*, ed. Roeland Harms, Joad Raymond, and Jeroen Salman (Leiden: Brill, 2013), 229–51.

[17] British Library, Add MS 4902, f. 48r-v; cf. Bulstrode Morton Whitelocke, *Journal of the Swedish Embassy in the Years 1653 and 1654*, vol. 1, ed. Charles Morton and Henry Reeve (London: John Edward Taylor, 1855), 205–6; see also Joad Raymond, 'Books as Diplomatic Agents: Milton in Sweden,' in *Cultures of Diplomacy and Literary Writing in the Early Modern World: New Approaches*, ed. Tracey A. Sowerby and Joanna Craigwood (Oxford: Oxford University Press, 2019), 131–45.

[18] Michiel van Groesen, *Amsterdam's Atlantic: Print Culture and the Making of Dutch Brazil* (Philadelphia: University of Pennsylvania Press, 2017), 190; Jacob Soll, *The Information Master: Jean-Baptiste Colbert's Secret State Intelligence System* (Ann Arbor: University of Michigan Press, 2009).

[19] Rosa Salzberg, *Ephemeral City: Cheap Print and Urban Culture in Renaissance Venice* (Manchester: Manchester University Press, 2014), 73–97.

effects. Vocabulary moves with material objects. This is essentially an improvisatory culture. The forms are then adapted to local culture – which includes language but also printing conventions.[20]

2.2.1 Mobility: Paragraphs

Another form of mobility lies in paragraphs. We repeatedly find the same paragraphs in different forms in different places and different languages. Using the same phrases, reordered and in different languages, makes the identity evident (this would provide an ideal test case for a project exploring polylingual text mining). The movement of these paragraphs means that Europe shares a news culture. News creates communities, and European politics is shaped by these communities.

The consequence of this new account of news history is that we must understand news as a fully European phenomenon, not merely as the agglomeration of regional cultures but as a fully transnational network, without which accounts of local histories will never be accurate.

2.2.2 Mobility: Corantos

One example of this is the movement of corantos from Amsterdam to London. Dutch language corantos appeared in Amsterdam in 1618 – the first was (probably) *Courante uyt Italien, Duytslandt, &c.* and was printed as a half-sheet folio in two columns.[21] This was a departure from the quarto pamphlet format typical of the Holy Roman Empire. Dutch corantos were gathered from manuscript and/or printed sources, mainly from the Netherlands and the Holy Roman Empire. Figure 1 maps the sources – that is, where the paragraphs of news come from – of the *Courante* for 1618–48.

The first English-language corantos were printed in the Netherlands and were translations of Dutch corantos. A Dutch engraver and bookseller named Petrus Keerius published the first in Amsterdam: a small, untitled

[20] Raymond and Moxham, *News Networks*, part one.

[21] Arthur der Weduwen, 'Competition, Choice and Diversity in the Newspaper Trade of the Dutch Golden Age,' *Early Modern Low Countries* 2 (2018): 7–23; Arthur der Weduwen, *Dutch and Flemish Newspapers of the Seventeenth Century, 1618–1700*, 2 vols. (Leiden: Brill, 2017).

Figure 1 Sources of printed news stories in the *Courante*, 1618–48.[22]

folio broadsheet in English – a form physically matching the Dutch equivalents. The earliest surviving issue, dated 2 December 1620, begins with the anticlimax: 'The new tydings out of Italie are not yet com.'[23] During 1620–1, London printers began to issue non-serial news pamphlets, which were translations of Dutch corantos, but in quarto format, matching the local conventions of news publication. Then, in 1621, Nathaniel Butter began to publish a translation of the Dutch *courante* and labelled it a coranto. Butter exactly imitated the Dutch form, contrary to London printing

---

[22] JR is indebted to the scholarly generosity of Arthur der Weduwen, who made available the entire database of his magnificent bibliography, *Dutch and Flemish Newspapers of the Seventeenth Century, 1618–1700*, as an Excel file, and to Yann Ryan for assisting him in analysing and mapping the data using Palladio, a software tool developed by the Humanities + Design labs at Stanford University for the visualisation of humanities data.

[23] Folke Dahl, *A Bibliography of English Corantos and Periodical Newsbooks 1620–1642* (London: Bibliographical Society, 1952), 31.

conventions. He formed a syndicate to publish these corantos, which spread commercial and perhaps legal risk, and in 1622 corantos began to appear in quarto format, matching English conventions. They were not, however, strictly periodical: issues appeared at intervals between two and eleven days.[24]

So the progression is as follows: Amsterdam corantos – Amsterdam printing of English translations of these corantos – London printing of English translations of Amsterdam corantos in Dutch-style format – London printing of English translation of Amsterdam corantos in English quarto format. This is a movement of both news and a news form which adapts to local conventions. The Dutch word also migrates into English. This is a characteristic pattern for the borrowing of printed forms. Note that the original Dutch coranto is probably taken from a mixture of printed and manuscript sources, and the idea for printing them may have been borrowed from the Holy Roman Empire (although it probably would have happened without the example set by Strasbourg in 1605). Hence the Dutch version fuses elements that originated elsewhere; Dutch activity transmitted Italian and German influences to London.

2.2.3 Mobility: Amboyna and the Anglo–Dutch Public Sphere

One of the effects of this level of international transaction was the creation of inter- or transnational communities – not only of consensus but also of conflict – which crossed political and ideological spaces. Helmer has proposed that there was an Anglo–Dutch public sphere, bridging the North Sea, languages, culture, and print commerce. A news event which demonstrates this was the controversy about the incident at Amboyna in 1623, when twenty men, ten of whom were members of the English East India Company, were tortured and executed for treason by representatives of the Dutch East India Company or VOC. The affair grew out of the companies' commercial rivalry in Indonesia and ended hopes of fostering cooperation between the two nations there and of British support for the Dutch Republic in the war against Spain.

---

[24] Joad Raymond, *Pamphlets and Pamphleteering in Early Modern Britain* (Cambridge: Cambridge University Press, 2003), 128–38.

There was a first flurry of news in 1623 in both Britain and the Netherlands, then another rush in 1632. One of the interesting characteristics of the exchange is the way that pamphlets incorporate translations of the enemy texts. The quotation of the antagonist is standard practice in animadversion, which since the Reformation had been a practice in pamphlet polemic (which can be contrasted with Scholastic methods, in which the counterarguments are invented rather than quoted).[25] This process of quotation and animadversion is distinctive in two respects, however. First, it involves translation, meaning that a fairly literal rendering of the original text is imported and made available to an audience who may well have been unable to access the original. This also creates Anglo–Dutch pamphlet exchange, which is sponsored by local publishers. London printers reproduce Dutch anti-English polemic. Second, the texts are incorporated in ways that preserve the physical appearance, perhaps the textual integrity, of the original editions.

A true relation of the unjust, cruell, and barbarous proceedings against the English at Amboyna was printed in London in 1624 (see Figure 2a). It contains three items: (1) the 'True Relation', (2) the 'copie of a Pamphlet, set forth first in Dutch and then in English, by some Neatherlander; falsely intituled, A True Declaration of the Newes that came out of the East-Indies', and (3) 'an Answer to the same Pamphlet. By the English East-India Company'. Together the three items run to over 100 pages, and therefore collectively they stretch the definition of a pamphlet: however, the second, Dutch item has a separate title page, and the distinct typography ameliorates the breach of conventions, making the triad look more like three conjoined pamphlets than a book. They are accompanied by a fourth item: a graphic woodcut depicting torture and killing (Figure 2b), sometimes bound before, and sometimes after, the title page. The printing is unusual: the signatures run consecutively, the pagination does not. Importantly, the typography of the incorporated Dutch pamphlet is different. The text block is a different size; the headers are in a different style.[26]

---

[25] Raymond, *Pamphlets and Pamphleteering*, 210–14.

[26] See https://books.google.co.uk/books?id=yoVmAAAAcAAJ&printsec (16 September 2022). Images (and more context) can be found at https://notevenpast.org/primary-source-pamphlets-propaganda-and-the-amboina-conspiracy-trial-in-the-classroom/ (28 February 2023).

(a)   (b)

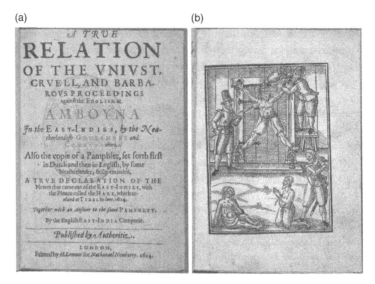

Figures 2a and b [John Skinner], *A true relation of the unjust, cruell, and barbarous proceedings against the English at Amboyna.* London: H[umphrey] Lownes (printer), Nathanael Newberry (editor), 1624 – Washington, DC: Folger Shakespeare Library, STC 7451 Copy 1; Digital Image Files 165078 and 64236 – Used by permission of the Folger Shakespeare Library under a Creative Commons Attribution-ShareAlike 4.0 International License.

The response to Amboyna has implications for our taxonomy, for the genetics of news mobility, and for how we see the relationship between news forms and news. But before we tease out our conclusions, we now turn to examine mobility and forms within France and the Holy Roman Empire.

2.3 Crossing Borders and Boundaries

The mobility of news in France and the Holy Roman Empire will be discussed with a focus on the French Wars of Religion, especially the years 1587 to 1590, when the production of news publications on the conflict reached a peak in France and the Holy Roman Empire. At this time, the Catholic League attempted to strengthen their position; their leaders who belonged to the Guise family were murdered by order of the king, and the last Valois king, Henry III, was himself murdered only months later; and Henry of Navarre, then Henry IV, seized power.

2.3.1 Crossing Borders – Connecting Regions

The German news publications on the French Wars of Religion were often compilations of visual and textual news-elements which can be traced in other news publications. Such news-elements or paragraphs generally moved from the region in which the reported events had happened to neighbouring regions with different languages and news markets: German pamphlets on the French Wars of Religion were in large part based on French manuscript and printed news publications which moved to the Empire in their entirety or as visual and textual news-elements.[27] The predominance of different languages in both regions was only a minor barrier: there was an audience in the Empire capable of reading news publications in French and, just as importantly, interested in news from their neighbour France. Peculiarities and special characteristics in the news markets of both regions were, of course, not only due to varying linguistic and cultural contexts but also due to different roles played by authorities, legal implications, and differing publishing contexts.[28]

German news publications on the French Wars of Religion characteristically established – or at least suggested – a close connection to the French news market: quite often, German pamphlets explicitly referred to a French original which a printing workshop had acquired; the text was adopted,

---

[27] The pamphlet *Außschreiben Kŏn: Mayestat inn Franckreich . . .* (Straßburg: Bernhard Jobin, 1589) combined three French news publications: *Declaration dv Roy svr la trefve . . .* (Tours: Jamet Mettayer, 1589), *EDIT DV ROY . . .* (Metz: Abraham Faber, 1589), and *Declaration dv Roy de Navarre . . .*, presumably by Philippe du Mornay (*s. l.*, 1589). Those French publications were published in a German translation in several pamphlets in the Empire. Compare Alexandra Schäfer-Griebel, *Die Medialität der Französischen Religionskriege. Frankreich und das Heilige Römische Reich 1589* (Stuttgart: Steiner, 2018), 286, n. 311.

[28] This is treated in Schäfer-Griebel, *Die Medialität*, *passim*.

translated, and sometimes commented on for the German news market.[29] References to the original French publications underlined the authenticity of the news and the transparency of the acquisition of information, the reliability of the presentation, and the proximity of the report and the events in France. While printers and publishers of pamphlets used the close connectedness to the French news market as a strategic advertising means, it was uncommon for German broadsheets and single-sheet prints to refer explicitly to French originals, even though re-uses of the image parts can be traced.[30]

While the news on recent events naturally trickled from France to its neighbours, the flow was not unidirectional. A few German news publications can be traced which were directed at a French audience and/or were adopted in France. The Cologne workshop of Franz Hogenberg, for example, produced French single-sheet prints, re-using the image parts of its printing plates, while the German textual part was eliminated or covered. Sometimes, the French text was simply placed alongside or beneath the German verses.

In addition, the Hogenberg workshop, which at that time had a unique role in the Holy Roman Empire in printing single sheets on the latest news, distributed German prints to France which were accompanied by sheets with French verses which were meant to be cut out and glued under the image of the single-sheet print.[31] Its single-sheet print *König Heinrich der*

---

[29] For example, *Indvciae. Frid vnd Anstand* (Frankfurt: Martin Lechler (printer), Paul Brachfeld (editor), 1589) explained on the title page that the translation of a Royal edict was included: 'Jtem/ Gemeltes Kŏnigs inn Franckreich Edict vnnd außschreiben'.

[30] The German single-sheet print *Ware conrafaiung Brueder Iacob Clements . . . (s. l.* [1589]) adopted a portrait of Jacques Clément, widely circulating in France in at least four versions: the engraving *F. Iaqves Clement (s. l.* [1589]), the woodcut *F. Iaqves Clement (s. l.* [1589]), *Le portraict de frere Iacques Clement . . .* ([Paris]: Antoine Du Brueil, [1589]), and *Histoire abregee de la vie de Henry de Valois . . .* (Paris: Pierre Mercier, 1589). The German single-sheet print took up the image but chose a neutral-descriptive title.

[31] Compare Hogenberg-Album, Paris: BNF, 4-QE-64 (A). On the practices of the Hogenberg workshop, compare Fritz Hellwig, 'Einleitung,' in *Franz Hogenberg / Abraham Hogenberg: Franz Hogenberg – Abraham Hogenberg. Geschichtsblätter*, ed. Fritz Hellwig (Nördlingen: Uhl 1983), 7–30, here 10; Alexandra Schäfer-Griebel,

Figure 3 Workshop of Franz Hogenberg (inventor and engraver), *König Heinrich der dritt des namen.* Cologne: workshop of Hogenberg (printer and editor), 1589; engraving – Munich: BSB, Res/4° Gall.g. 302 f-1 Historia, https://mdz-nbn-resolving.de/urn:nbn:de:bvb:12-bsb00026283-3 (21 September 22) – https://creativecommons.org/licenses/by-nc-sa/4.0/

dritt (Figure 3) seems to have been the starting point for a French series of sixteen single-sheet prints on the murder of Henry III, entitled *Année 1589*. Hogenberg's high-quality etching from 1589 was cut into four individual images. The textual part from the sheet was placed under two of the images, and thereby the narrative sequence of the German original was changed: the first two paragraphs with German verses from the single-sheet print *König Heinrich der dritt* were placed under the image of Navarre's succession to the

'Les guerres de religion en France dans les gravures de Hogenberg' in *Médialité et interprétation contemporaine des premières guerres de Religion*, ed. Lothar Schilling and Gabriele Haug-Moritz (Berlin: De Gruyter, 2014), 98–120.

French crown in the series *Année 1589*. The other German verses and the French prose text which accompanied the image of the punishment of the regicide in *König Heinrich der dritt* were regrouped in the series *Année 1589*: there, the text was placed under the image of the assassination of King Henry III by the monk Jacques Clément.[32] Another twelve etchings whose quality fell behind were added without a textual part but with a few image captions. The artistic style as well as the clothing suggest that some sheets were contemporary (i.e. late sixteenth century) and others were added later in the seventeenth century. Consequently, it remains uncertain precisely when the compilation of this French series of single-sheet prints took place.

To envision the close connectedness of both regions and their news markets, it can also help to focus on media events. One example could be the defeat of the German auxiliary campaign of 1587. When the campaign led by Fabian von Dohna for Johann Casimir, the main German supporter of the French Protestants, saw a crushing defeat, the German side and the French Protestant leader Henry of Navarre disagreed who was responsible. Both sides blamed the other's failures, and each responded to the other's accusations.[33] Manuscript publications, pamphlets, and single-sheet prints circulated in German, French, and Latin in France and the Holy Roman Empire alike.[34] The pamphlet *Erklärung / Auß was*

---

[32] Compare *König Heinrich der dritt des namen* (Cologne: workshop of Franz Hogenberg, 1589); *Année 1589. Autre Histoire de Jacques Clément . . . (s. l.* s. d.).

[33] Compare Ruth Kohlndorfer, *Diplomatie und Gelehrtenrepublik. Die Kontakte des französischen Gesandten Jacques Bongars (1554–1612)* (Tübingen: Max Niemeyer, 2009), 50–1; Fabian von Dohna, *Die Selbstbiographie des Burggrafen Fabian zu Dohna (1550–1621) nebst Aktenstücken zur Geschichte der Sukzession der Kurfürsten von Brandenburg in Preussen aus dem fürstlich dohnaischen Hausarchive zu Schlobitten*, ed. Christian Krollmann (Leipzig: Duncker & Humblot, 1905), 112.

[34] Compare Dohna, *Selbstbiographie*, 112–15. Publications from 1587 and 1588 on the military campaign by Dohna: VD16 ZV 2255, VD16 ZV 30822, VD16 ZV 16588, VD16 ZV 11385, VD16 K 2693. Concerning *avvisi* and *Zeitungsbriefe* in 1587, compare Cornel A. Zwierlein, *Discorso und Lex Dei. Die Entstehung neuer Denkrahmen im 16. Jahrhundert und die Wahrnehmung der französischen Religionskriege in Italien und Deutschland* (Göttingen: Vandenhoeck & Ruprecht, 2006), 773 with n. 590.

Vrsachen,[35] for example, presented an explanation by Henry of Navarre translated from Latin into German as well as the justification of Jacques de Ségur-Pardaillan, the ambassador of Navarre in the Empire. Furthermore, the pamphlet included the defence of the German military leaders written by Fabian von Dohna. Finally, several reports were included from various military camps in France. All those texts were listed on the title page (Figure 4). This combination of already-circulating texts made them available for a broader audience through resumption, printing, and translation. As the participants in this publicly conducted debate had different authoritative status, they contributed in different communication channels, text forms, and media, reaching out to differing but overlapping audiences while still reacting and responding to each other. A shared French–German public sphere existed at that time and lasted at least for the limited period of the ongoing discussion.

2.3.2 Crossing Media Boundaries – Intermediality and Co-dependency

The use and sometimes combination of French manuscript and printed sources were standard in German news publications. Sometimes, French or German oral sources for news publications can be traced as well.[36] The German ballad *Ein Schön new Lied von dem Nauarrischen Höer zug von Schweyzeren Reütteren vnd Landsknechts*, on the German auxiliary campaign from 1587, can be traced back to Catholic Switzerland in 1590.[37] Such ballads were written down on separate manuscript sheets and added to German *avvisi* – in this case, to the *Fuggerzeitungen*.[38] Their character as immediate oral, performative statements in the conflict changed with the

---

[35] Compare Henry of Navarre, Jacques de Ségur-Pardaillan Fabian von Dohna et al., *Erklärung/ Auß was Vrsachen . . . .* (*s. l.* 1587).

[36] Compare the remark on oral sources in *Drey Warhafftige newe Zeitung. Aus Franckreich . . .* (Basel: Samuel Apiarius, 1589).

[37] Compare Oswald Bauer, *Pasquille in den Fuggerzeitungen. Spott- und Schmähgedichte zwischen Polemik und Kritik (1568–1605)* (Munich: Böhlau, 2008), 186.

[38] Compare Bauer, *Pasquille*, 201, n. 17.

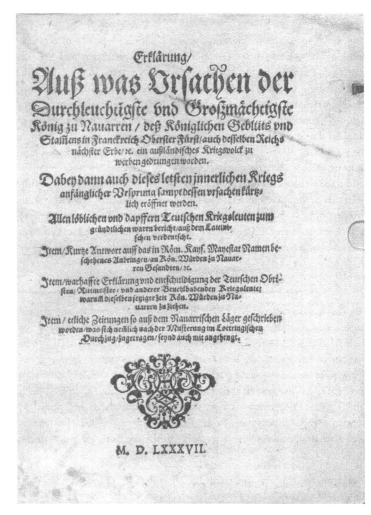

Erklärung/

Auß was Vrsachen der

Durchleuchtigste vnd Großmächtigste

König zu Nauarren / deß Königlichen Geblüts vnd
Stammens in Franckreich Oberster Fürst/ auch desselben Reichs
nächster Erbe/ ꝛc. ein außländisches Kriegsvolck zu
werben gedrungen worden.

Dabey dann auch dieses letsten innerlichen Kriegs
anfänglicher Vrsprung sampt dessen vrsachen kürtz-
lich eröffnet werden.

Allen löblichen vnd dapffern Teutschen Kriegsleuten zum
gründtlichen waren bericht/ auß dem Lateini-
schen verdeutscht.

Item/ Kurtze Antwort auff das in Röm. Kayf. Mayestat Namen be-
schehenes Anbringen/ an Kön. Würden zu Nauar-
ren Gesandten/ ꝛc.

Item/ warhaffte Erklärung vnd entschuldigung der Teutschen Obri-
sten/ Rittmeister/ vnd anderer Beuelhabenden Kriegsleutet
warumb dieselben setziger zeit Kön. Würden zu Nauarren zu ziehen.

Item/ etliche Zeitungen so auß dem Nauarrischen Läger geschrieben
worden/ was sich nemlich nach der Musterung im Lottringischen
Durchzug/ zugetragen/ seynd auch mit angehengt.

M. D. LXXXVII.

Figure 4 Henry of Navarre, Jacques de Ségur-Pardaillan, Fabian von Dohna
et al., *Erklärung/ Auß was Vrsachen . . . s. l.* 1587 – Munich: BSB, Gall.g. 1024 y,
https://mdz-nbn-resolving.de/urn:nbn:de:bvb:12-bsb00038024-1
(21 September 2022). https://creativecommons.org/licenses/by-nc-sa/4.0/

change of media and news form, when the geographical reach broadened through written dissemination. Infrequently, German handwritten *avvisi* or German printed pamphlets, or even less frequently newsletters and manuscript separates, were taken up either entirely or in part.[39] News moved between different news forms and crossed media boundaries. In the pamphlet *Warhaffte vnd eigentiche Beschreibung*, for example, the first part of the text was identical to the manuscript news sheet *Bericht des König*, which in large part was also taken up in the pamphlet *Zeyttung*. In addition, *Warhaffte vnd eigentliche Beschreibung* combined the aforementioned account of events with a prophecy which can also be found in the pamphlet *Wunderbärlicher Abschiedt*.[40] Even though we know the French original for this pamphlet, the prophecy was not part of it.[41] Despite including recycled visual and textual news-elements, many news publications remained a unique product in the way those news-elements were combined and compiled.

The different origins of news-elements were perceptible in many news publications because different types of text, writing styles and typographies, and ways of representing and depicting the events visually as well as

---

[39] For example, *New Zeytung Auß Franckreich* . . . (Cologne: Gottfried von Kempen, 1589) and *Newe Zeitung aus Franckreich* (*s. l.*, 1589) showed the identical text as the manuscript separate *Waher vnd wie sich, die Erschröcklich Mörderrey, Jetz verschinen. 23. vnd 24. December. A[nn]o: 88. Jn Franckhreich zvegetragen.* which had been inserted in a *Fuggerzeitung* (*s. l. s. d.*, Codex 8961, ff. 915v–917v). On travel and acquisition of information on the French Wars of Religion in German printing workshops, compare Alexandra Schäfer-Griebel, 'Die Arbeitspraxis im Nachrichtendruckgewerbe. Religionskriegsnachrichten im Heiligen Römischen Reich um 1590,' *Jahrbuch für Kommunikationsgeschichte* 20 (2018): 42–70, here 53–9.

[40] Compare *Warhaffte vnd eigentliche Beschreibung / dern Historia* . . . (Cologne: Nikolaus Schreiber, 1589); *Zeyttung Auß Franckreich* . . . (Augsburg: Josias Wörli, 1589); *Bericht des König in Franckreichs zugefügter entleibung* in *Fuggerzeitungen, s. l.*, 26 August 1589, Codex 8962, ff. 248r/492r–250v/494v; *Wunderbärlicher Abschiedt / vnd seltzamer Todt / Henrici des dritten* . . . (*s. l.* 1589).

[41] Compare *Admirable et prodigievse mort de Henry de Valoys* . . . (Paris: Pierre Des Hayes, 1589).

positionings vis-à-vis the French conflict were combined in one publication. On multi-lingual single-sheet prints, a pro-League interpretation in French, favouring the actions taken by Clément, could stand alongside a pro-Royal interpretation in German. In this way, different readings of recent events dominating in both regions were combined in one news publication (cf. Figure 7).[42] Some printing workshops seem to have compiled every available material without investing much time, effort, and money into reworking the entire publications or news-elements which they re-used. They aimed to maximise their economic profit thanks to rising interest in the Empire in what happened in the French Wars of Religion.[43] In other cases, it is obvious that the selection, combination, and re-working of news depended on the religious and political background of the authors, printers, and publishers whose news communications showed a sometimes apparent or sometimes hidden agenda.[44] Some news people, however, made serious efforts to present an elaborate and rounded news publication and therefore bundled different and sometimes contradictory views together (e.g. *Erklärung/ Auß was Vrsachen*).

It has already been argued that news – often in the form of visual and textual news-elements – crossed boundaries of media and news forms. As media performed slightly different roles for partly distinct though overlapping audiences, some designed their publications with the co-dependency of news forms in mind: it was presumably the Straßburg workshop of Bernhard Jobin which published the pamphlet *Königliche Declaration Erzehlung*,[45] a compilation of several texts, combined with an enclosed single-sheet print at the end which also circulated independently.[46] The workshop not only added captions and referred to the image throughout

---

[42] Compare *König Heinrich der dritt.*

[43] Compare Schäfer-Griebel, 'Die Arbeitspraxis,' 61–2.

[44] On the importance of the personal background of individual 'news people,' compare Schäfer-Griebel, 'Die Arbeitspraxis,' 49.

[45] Compare *Königliche Declaration Erzehlung* ... (Straßburg: Bernhard Jobin?, 1589).

[46] Compare *Auszlegüng Vnd bedeütüng hierin stehender ziefren findet man Klärlich im Trück Königliche Declaration intitüliret* (s. l. 1589).

the text (in the part headed *Ursachen*) but also augmented the text with a few sentences which modified incongruences between the image and textual components. The workshop intended that pamphlet and single-sheet print be purchased together, providing different but complementary views.

The co-dependency of news forms can be traced not only in individual news publications. While reports on the military campaigns were among the most common printed publications in France, hardly any printed publications in the Empire were dedicated to military issues in 1588–89.[47] However, military campaigns were among the central topics in *avvisi* circulating in the Empire,[48] so that news on certain topics appears to have been available exclusively in one news form, which was clearly meant to be received together with other news communication.

Which news forms complemented each other varied in the different regions – not least because the spectrum of news forms differed. Exclusive newsletters about the French Wars of Religion, written by agents in exchange for a fee, were available in France but were unusual in the Empire because they were too expensive and laborious.[49] In contrast, *avvisi*, circulated widely in the Empire but were not yet available in France. Handwritten serial news sheets emerged only in the last period of the

---

[47] Compare Schäfer-Griebel, *Die Medialität*, i.a. 164, 180; Michel Cassan, 'La guerre en discours. L'année 1589 en France,' in *Le bruit des armes. Mises en formes et désinformations en Europe pendant les guerres de Religion (1560–1610)*, ed. Jérémie Foa and Paul-Alexis Mellet (Paris: Honoré Champion, 2012), 259–75, here 261.

[48] One German reader of manuscript military accounts of the French Wars of Religion was Georg Kölderer, *Beschreibunng vnd Kurtze Vertzaichnis Fürnemer Lob vnnd gedenckhwürdiger Historien. Eine Chronik der Stadt Augsburg der Jahre 1576 bis 1607*, vol. 3: 1589–1593 (Codex S 43), ed. Wolfgang E. J. Weber with Silvia Strodel (Augsburg: Wißner-Verlag, 2013), i.a. 1229, 1232, 1234, 1236, 1244.

[49] Compare Cornel A. Zwierlein, 'Komparative Kommunikationsgeschichte und Kulturtransfer im 16. Jahrhundert. Methodische Überlegungen entwickelt am Beispiel der Kommunikation über die französischen Religionskriege (1559–1598) in Deutschland und Italien,' in *Kulturtransfer. Kulturelle Praxis im 16. Jahrhundert*, ed. Wolfgang Schmale (Innsbruck: De Gruyter, 2003), 85–120, here 97, 103.

French Wars of Religion when Henry IV was broadly accepted as king and a functioning postal system was re-established which allowed a regular transfer of news.[50] Political and communicational instability had prevented the adoption of serial news sheets in France at an earlier stage. In a German collection, that of the Heidelberg court, early French serial news sheets from 1595 to 1596 survive.[51] These French news sheets show some of the characteristics of the existing German or Italian examples, such as the regularity of dissemination or the standard form, but they did not yet appear periodically.[52] Nevertheless, the intense French-German-Italian political and communicational relations which were supported during the French Wars of Religion provided the framework for the transfer of *avvisi* as a news form; in turn, the framework was enabled by the interlocking of news networks in different geographical areas.[53]

2.4 Dancing across Europe

News forms have commanded too much of our attention. We've demonstrated this by gathering a variety of forms that spread across much of Europe and showing them to be overlapping, multi-valent, and mobile. If we want to understand how news forms work, we have to stop thinking in terms of news forms and instead think about news in motion, as something that is fundamentally *fungible* and as something that fosters and cements

---

[50] Compare François Moureau, *Répertoire des nouvelles à la main. Dictionnaire de la presse manuscrite clandestine XVIe–XVIIIe siècle* (Oxford: Voltaire Foundation, 1999), X–XI, 3 (catalogue).

[51] Those first French serial news sheets of 1595 and 1596 – among others – were spread through royal diplomatic contacts: The agents of the French king, Jacques Bongars and Guillaume Ancel, negotiated with the count Palatine Frederick IV about support for the royal party. *Avvisi* dating from 25 December 1595 to 11 April 1596 were included in the dossier on the German–French negotiations. The serial news sheets reported especially about the struggle for power in France taking sides for Henry IV (cf. Moureau, *Répertoire des nouvelles à la main*, 3).

[52] Compare Moureau, *Répertoire des nouvelles à la main*, X–XI.

[53] On the cultural transfer of news in the context of French-German-Italian contacts and in relation to the French Wars of Religion, compare Zwierlein, *Discorso und Lex Dei*, *passim*.

social processes and interactions.[54] By focusing on the mobility of news and searching for transmission processes, we can apprehend and even measure the connectiveness of different geographical areas. This should not obscure the fact that news in different areas showed peculiarities and distinctive characteristics. However, the wider network is shared, the news is commonly the same or similar, and the forms are cognate. While we must abandon the tyranny of printed forms, it is nonetheless possible, and hopefully useful, to draw up a taxonomy of news forms (see www.cambridge.org/communicatingthenews), in part because the names and the conventions of those forms move around Europe with the news itself. But we need to be careful of *faux amis* because these forms and words underwent subtle transformations to adapt to local cultural conventions.

When news travelled from a local to a regional or even broader setting, this could imply a change of news form or communication channel (from oral to manuscript to print and back again) in the process of transmitting, translating, and re-working. Ballads were written down so they could be more widely distributed, and *avvisi* and manuscript separates, to name only two examples, served as models for printed publications. It was not only texts that travelled across geographical and media boundaries but visual news-elements as well. Not only did entire news publications move, but so too did small units in a variety of forms such as news stories, paragraphs, parts of figures, and fragments. The different origins of those small news units compiled in one publication were often perceptible because components with different genres, styles, typography, ways of representing, and partisanship stood alongside one another, especially in print publications. We have seen that the visibility of (different) models in printed news publications was not due simply to a lack of effort; rather, the close connectedness to the French news market served as a strategical, advertising means ('authenticity') for the German news publications. When news changed during the process of transmission into a different geographical area, conventions for selecting news, deeply rooted in local habit and

---

[54] Daniel Bellingradt, Paul Nelles, and Jeroen Salman, eds., *Books in Motion in Early Modern Europe: Beyond Production, Circulation and Consumption* (London: Macmillan, 2017).

custom, played a major role, alongside those played by authority, legal implications, and publishing contexts. At the same time, the practice of selecting, compiling, and re-working depended heavily on the background, both political and religious, of authors, printers, and publishers. Even news forms which appear to be non-partial and informative often had a hidden agenda. However, many news persons, and especially the printing work-shops, showed pragmatism (e.g. using all the space on a sheet) and prioritised the maximising of profit with minimal effort. While foreign news was usually less partial, it could become more engaged when the neighbour was politically, diplomatically, or militarily involved, as in the case of the German auxiliary troops in 1587. Both sides criticised the other's failures in a variety of text genres, addressed at slightly different audiences, published in different languages, but nevertheless participating in the same debate, reacting and responding to each other. Then a real exchange of news created a mutual – even though contestatory – public sphere for a limited period of time.

News usually travelled from the geographical area where something took place to neighbouring countries with an audience capable of and interested in reading those news – in a foreign language or in translation. This flow of news was not exclusively unidirectional but rather asymmetrical, as foreign reports on home news were adopted as well. Of course, the postal system played a major role in the transport of news and the connection of different geographical areas across borders.

The example of Amboyna presses upon the taxonomy we have presented and upon our main contention that news needs to be thought of beyond forms. It shows news being recycled with different ends in mind, engaging contexts in different ways. A national public sphere is not sufficient to explain the debate, the politics, and the political identities deployed here. The focus on exchanges allows us to see how the close relation of neigh-bouring countries favoured the adoption of a new news form which was already established in one area when the necessary preconditions existed (functioning postal system; *avvisi* appear in France).

Moreover, the Amboyna example shows something of the deeper structures of the texts and their development and social uses: it is a clear example of bundling. Bundling, a central and overlooked aspect of early modern news culture, is the practice of assembling multiple items together to make a composite and rounded news communication. News readers consumed *avvisi* alongside separates and pamphlets, and this aggregation was systematic and fundamental to reading practices. Which media were designed and read – with co-dependency in mind – depended on the spectrum of available news, which varied by region. In the Empire, *avvisi* on military campaigns in France were read alongside other news publications on different aspects of the French Wars of Religion to obtain a comprehensive picture of the latest events. In France, the news forms differed from those of the Empire and therefore the practices and products of bundling differed. The two Amboyna items described above can be found bound together with a third, *The stripping of Ioseph, or The crueltie of brethren to a brother In a sermon . . . With a consolatorie epistle, to the English-East-India Companie, for their vnsufferable wrongs sustayned in Amboyna, by the Dutch there*, printed in London in 1625. The sermon is also concerned with the Amboyna incident. At least one reader literally bundled these pamphlets together, taking them to a binder to be physically joined. News media are co-dependent in design. News is never written to be complete or comprehensive: one of the defining qualities of all news genres is that they must be bundleable.

3 News Sings

3.1 Introduction

This section moves beyond the written and printed word, which for a long time have been the object of study of the histories of early modern European news. Until recently, the aural dimension in the news circulation has been neglected by historians in favour of the textual and the written. *The Invention of News* illustrated how in pre-modern European information culture, despite the widespread circulation of commercial manuscripts newsletters, *avvisi* and printed pamphlets, news mostly 'passed by word of mouth', through conversations, poems, sermons, official announcements, and ballads or songs.[55] All over Europe, much of the population (literate and illiterate) learned the news by hearing it from preachers, heralds, or street singers.

In this section, we focus on a specific medium in the aural circulation of information: the news ballad or news song.[56] We compare actors, publics, music, and soundscapes of news singing in European cities. We highlight similarities and differences in immaterial elements such as sound, music, and voice, which played a central role in the dissemination of news. Singing was a powerful communicative tool that was particularly effective for amplifying news and opinions precisely because of its performative and multi-media character. In cities from Copenhagen to Lisbon, from London to Naples, news ballads were sung, heard, rehearsed, and sung again in markets, taverns, streets, and squares because their verses were set to common, well-known tunes that helped listeners to memorise and pass on information. Political poems, sensationalist news ballads, celebratory verses, and protest songs may be viewed as multi-media and performative public acts, as we try to imagine how these works – and the information

---

[55] Andrew Pettegree, *The Invention of News: How the World Came to Know About Itself* (New Haven: Yale University Press, 2014).

[56] On methodological challenges, see Una McIlvenna, 'When the News was Sung: Ballads as News Media in Early Modern Europe,' *Media History* 22, nos. 3–4 (2016): 317–33; Jenni Hyde, *Singing the News: Ballads in Mid-Tudor England* (Abingdon: Routledge, 2018).

they circulated – might have sounded to sixteenth-century ears. Cheaply printed and sold in markets, streets, and squares, anonymously circulated in manuscript, posted at night on church walls, or read aloud and performed in public spaces of urban sociability, ephemeral news ballads exerted an acoustic, musical, and mnemonic power that enhanced their communicative impact on early modern information culture. A common characteristic of European news ballads was precisely their fluid mobility between different media – sonic, verbal, visual, gestural, and written. They were part of a complex communication system, dominated by a high level of intermediality.[57]

In addition to emphasising the powers of sound and song in the circulation of information, we advocate a non-elitist conception of the news business, considering news as a commodity intended for a wide and diverse audience, not as the patrimony of members of functional elites.[58] In terms of production, dissemination, and reception, news singing crossed social and cultural barriers. Different political and social actors (ranging from cardinals and diplomats to friars and merchants, from street performers to humanists, and from milkmaids to cobblers) populated a heterogeneous pre-modern public sphere and made ample use of the news ballad as a source of information.[59]

3.2 Printing and Selling News Ballads

The material evidence of constant interaction between different media in the circulation of information is provided by the many news songs that have survived through printed editions. In England, topical songs took the form of broadside ballads, printed in multiple columns of black-letter type on a single side of a folio of rough paper. They might include decorative borders and woodcut illustrations to make the sheet visually appealing. Both in Italy and Spain, popular news songs also had common, recognisable formats – cheaply printed pamphlets in quarto or octavo, usually of fewer

---

[57] On this concept, see Bellingradt and Rospocher, *The Intermediality of Early Modern Communication*.

[58] Heiko Droste, *The Business of News* (Leiden-Boston: Brill 2021).

[59] Rospocher, *Beyond the Public Sphere*.

than eight pages, with a single illustration on the first page. The titles were printed in larger fonts that anticipated the content. Woodcuts were often re-used, usually with care to ensure that the chosen image suited the words of the ballad,[60] but sometimes the need for quick and cheap production prompted printers to make hasty choices. The latter was the case in an Italian news song dedicated to the siege and fall of Rhodes (1522), whose frontispiece was accompanied by a recycled woodcut of the city of Padua.[61] Norwegian skilling (shilling) songs, so called because of their price, were also printed as pamphlets of four or eight pages.[62] German *Lieder* were less well defined, printed as either quarto pamphlets or single sheets. The size of the sheet varied, and they could include several or no images; the text appeared in one, two, or three columns, usually with a headline. Often they indicated their news form explicitly as *Lied, Gesang*, or *Weise*.[63] Dutch and French songs printed on broadsides were often reprinted in songbooks (*recueils*). The format of the medium to some extent dictated how singers performed and sold their wares on the street.[64]

---

[60] Christopher Marsh, 'A Woodcut and Its Wanderings in Seventeenth-Century England,' *Huntington Library Quarterly* 79, no. 2 (2016): 245–62.

[61] *El sanguinolento & incendioso assedio del gran turcho contra el christianissimo Rodo. Con epistola del gran turcho a Rodi: et de epsi al gran turcho responsiua in latino prosa tersissima* [Venice c. 1526], c. 2ʳ. On this pamphlet and more in general on the recycling of images, see Massimo Rospocher and Rosa Salzberg, *Il mercato dell'informazione. Notizie vere, false e sensazionali nella Venezia del Cinquecento* (Venice: Marsilio 2022), 62–4.

[62] Siv Gøril Brandtzæg, 'Skillingsvisene i Norge 1550–1950: Historien om et forsømt forskningsfelt/Broadside Ballads in Norway 1550–1950: The Story of an Overlooked Research Field,' *Edda* 105, no. 2 (2018): 93–109, here 96.

[63] Rolf Wilhelm Brednich, *Die Liedpublizistik im Flugblatt des 15. bis 17. Jahrhunderts*, 2 vols. (Baden-Baden: Koerner, 1974–5); Stephanie Moisi, 'Das politische Lied der Reformationszeit (1517–1555). Ein Beitrag zur Kommunikationsgeschichte des Politischen 16. Jahrhundert' (PhD diss., Graz, 2015).

[64] Una McIlvenna, *Singing the News of Death: Execution Ballads in Europe 1500–1900* (Oxford: Oxford University Press, 2022), 8; Moisi, 'Das politische Lied der Reformationszeit.'

These ephemeral items were amongst the cheapest printed material available. In Venice, the price was only a quarter of a *soldo* at the end of the fifteenth century, when the daily salary of a worker at the Arsenale was six *soldi*.[65] In Oxford, broadside ballads were sold for half a penny in 1520, when the daily wage of a labourer was about four pence.[66] English broadside ballads cost a penny by the end of the sixteenth century, but this was still affordable for most people at least occasionally. We can imagine that at the end of a performance, the street singers would turn to the audience for payment for the performance or for the sale of the print. Allusions to the aural dimension remain evident in printed texts, which contain ritual expressions that hint at the commercial, gestural, or performative dynamics of this exchange. The Ferrarese street singer Bighignol ended his verse account of a Venetian military defeat along the Po river with a reference to the payment for his performance: 'Whoever wants the story that I sing from the bench, / ... let him bring the money and he shall have it'.[67] The same happened with the sixteenth-century printer-perfomer Niccolò Zoppino, who closed his news ballad on the same battle with a request to be paid: 'if you want this *frotelina* [...] put your hand in your pocket / dig out two *quattrini* / and place [them] in the hands of Niccolò Zoppino'.[68]

The heyday of the Italian printed news ballad, the early sixteenth century, was rather earlier than that of topical songs elsewhere in Europe. Cities like Venice represented early communication and information hubs,

---

[65] Salzberg, *Ephemeral City*.

[66] John Dorne, 'The Daily Ledger of John Dorne, 1520,' in *Collectanea*, First Series, ed. F. Madan (Oxford: Oxford Historical Society at the Clarendon Press, 1885), 171–8; E. H. Phelps Brown and Sheila V. Hopkins, 'Seven Centuries of Building Wages,' *Economica*, New Series 22, no. 87 (1955): 296–314, here 198.

[67] Bighignol, *Li horrendi e magnanimi fatti de l'ilustrissimo Alfonso duca di Ferrara contra l'armata de venetiani in Po del mile e cinque cento e noue del mese de decembre a giorni uintidoi* (Ferrara: Baldassare Selli, 1510), f. 2v.

[68] Niccolò Zoppino, *Barzoleta novamente composta de la mossa facta per venetiani contra alo ilustrissimo Signore Alphonso duca terzo de Ferrara* (Ferrara c. 1509), f. 2v.

urban public spaces where a news marketplace rapidly developed.[69] In fact, Venice was exceptional for the 'speed and scale of [the] initial explosion' of print which both drew on and passed into oral circulation of news.[70] Printed material of this sort did not reach Norway until the mid-seventeenth century. Although this did not prevent skilling songs from circulating there prior to the arrival of print, it was during the seventeenth and eighteenth centuries that they functioned as a source of news for the common people, especially those who could not read.[71]

Throughout much of Europe, news ballads continued to circulate even after the creation of a reliably periodical press. At times, they contained stories not carried in the newspapers of the day.[72] At other times, ballads offered their audience not breaking news but a commentary on events in a more or less recent past. In Italy, well into the twentieth century, ballad singers were still active with an informative function; for instance, in the squares, they performed ballads on the execution of dictator Benito Mussolini in 1945, or outside factories, they recited the latest news on the political protests of the 1970s.

3.3 News Singing

European news ballads were intended to be sung and heard. The fact that balladeers across Europe made a living from singing as well as selling these songs should suggest that they were capable performers who managed to appeal to their audience. In a society reliant on face-to-face transmission for news and information, ballad consumers often learned the melodies (and perhaps the words) from the singer's performance. This would have been impossible if the balladeer merely chanted tunelessly. Some tunes were

---

[69]　Massimo Rospocher and Rosa Salzberg, *Il mercato dell'informazione. Notizie vere, false e sensazionali nella Venezia del Cinquecento* (Venice: Marsilio 2022); Peter Burke, 'Early Modern Venice as a Center of Information and Communication,' in *Venice Reconsidered: The History and Civilisation of an Italian City-State*, ed. John Jeffries Martin and Dennis Romano (London: Johns Hopkins University Press, 2000), 389–419.

[70]　Salzberg, *Ephemeral City*, 7.

[71]　Brandtzæg, *Skillingsvisene i Norge*, 96–7.

[72]　*Ibid.*, 100.

complicated in both metre and pitch movement, which suggests that while many ballad singers probably had little or no professional musical training, they had significant musical ability. It was common for street singers to be skilled instrumentalists: during their apprenticeship, blind performers in Spain could also be trained to play the guitar or the violin, while street singers in Italy were often excellent players of stringed instruments like the *lira* or *viola da braccio*.[73] Some of them were so proficient that they took their name from their instrument, as in the case of an early sixteenth-century performer from Urbino, Vincenzo Citaredo ('guitarist'). Fiddles, pipes, and drums were probably the most common accompaniments to English ballads.

Nowhere in Europe did the ballad rely on the ability of the audience to read music or even printed words. Combining rhymes with appealing and easily remembered tunes and music made news songs more memorable and allowed them to spread well beyond those who could read. For example, sometimes the titles of early modern Spanish war ballads indicate their tunes with the epigraph to be sung 'to the tune of'. This is the case of the *Cançó de la victòria de Montjuïc al to del fara lara la* ('Per tot lo món se conta'), from 1641, or the *Cançó al to de l'estudiant, i de la tristesa del lleó i victòria de Flix* ('Dem gràcies al Senyor'), from 1645.[74] As a rule, the most popular ballad tunes tended to be the musically simpler ones.[75] In early modern Italy, these were frequently repetitive melodies that served as a musical basis for the performer's improvisation or semi-improvisation. Large numbers of English tunes survive, usually in arrangements for lute or virginals.[76] Often tunes circulated Europe. From 1600 onwards, increasing numbers

---

[73] Blake Wilson, 'The *Cantastorie/Canterino/Cantimbanco* as Musician,' *Italian Studies* 71, no. 2 (2016): 154–70.

[74] Eulàlia Miralles, 'Versos efímeros para la guerra de Separación catalana,' *Bibliofilia* 121, no. 2 (2019): 313–28, here 325.

[75] Christopher Marsh, '"Fortune My Foe": The Circulation of an English Super-Tune,' in *Identity, Intertextuality, and Performance in Early Modern Song Culture*, ed. Dieuwke van der Poel, Louis Grijp, and Wim van Anrooij (Leiden: Brill, 2016), 312–13.

[76] William Chappell, *Popular Music of the Olden Time*, 2 vols. (London: Cramer, Beale and Chappell, 1855); Claude Simpson, *The British Broadside Ballad and its Music* (New Brunswick: Rutgers University Press, 1966).

of French and English tunes appear as the melodies for Dutch songs.[77] Indeed, little new music was composed in the Dutch Republic. Instead, ballads relied on imported tunes.[78] One popular English ballad tune, 'Fortune My Foe', was used for 272 Dutch songs and was found in French and German scores.[79]

Unlike those from other European contexts, Italian news ballads do not usually identify their tunes, nor do many melodies survive. However, it seems that appropriate melodies for certain verse or metric forms were familiar enough to audiences not to need specification. The Italian performers' core repertoire were *cantari*, improvised (or semi-improvised) vernacular narrative songs in *ottava rima*. Like English ballads, Italian *cantari* could be used to recount both secular and sacred stories, fantasy, history, and mostly recent events. Street singers also used other metres: *barzellette* or *frottole* were shorter songs used to deliver more direct political messages and to promote audience participation (usually with an easy refrain or repeated lines, which allowed the publics to join in).

Balladeers frequently cashed in on the popularity of tunes by re-using them for new words in a process known as contrafactum. English ballad tunes at times even added meaning to the song by being re-used for songs on similar themes.[80] Many English crime ballads were set to 'Fortune my Foe', while a common tune for Dutch crime ballads was 'O Holland Schoon

---

[77] Dieuwke van der Poel, 'Exploring Love's Options: Song and Youth Culture in the Sixteenth Century Netherlands,' in *Identity, Intertextuality, and Performance*, 229.

[78] Louis Grijp, *Het Nederlandse Lied in de Gouden Eeuw* (Amsterdam: Meertens Institute, 1991), 322.

[79] *Dutch Song Database*, www.liederenbank.nl/resultaatlijst.php?zoekveld=greensleeves&submit=search&enof=EN-zoeken&zoekop=allewoordenlied&sorteer=jaar&lan=en&wc=true (accessed 26 September 2022); Una McIlvenna, *Singing the News of Death*, 62. See also Marsh, 'Fortune My Foe'.

[80] Christopher Marsh, *Music and Society in Early Modern England* (Oxford: Oxford University Press, 2012); Hyde, *Singing the News*; McIlvenna, 'When the News Was Sung'; Una McIlvenna, 'The Rich Merchant Man, or, What the Punishment of Greed Sounded Like in Early Modern English Ballads,' *Huntington Library Quarterly* 79, no. 2 (2016): 279–99; Una McIlvenna, 'The Power of Music: the

gij leeft in vrede'; these 'hanging tunes' gained a particular association with execution.[81] 'Fortune' was identified as a particularly 'godly' tune by Tessa Watt, and arguably the tune alone encouraged 'listener-singers to reflect upon the spiritual nature of the execution process, and to contemplate their own sinful lives'.[82] As such, these songs 'can only be understood in the light of their models, for that is how a contemporary listener would have understood them'.[83] Sometimes tunes were so popular that even when a melody was not named, the audience could identify it from the stanza pattern and rhyme scheme of the words.[84]

European ballads contain many references to the performative and oral transmission of the texts. Strong narratives were central to the oral tradition and were clearly suited to popular news songs. The frequent use of simple rhythms and rhetorical devices such as rhyme, repetition, and alliteration points to both the oral origins of the genre and the continued importance of the oral transmission of printed texts. In Venice, there was a close association between performance and the sale of printed materials by the sixteenth century.[85] Likewise, in a text related to the discovery of the New World, which recasts the letter of Christopher Columbus, the Florentine Giuliano Dati constantly addresses an audience of listeners. The word *auditore* ('listener') appears throughout, and at the end, Dati explicitly mentions a crowd of 'Magnificent and kind people, gathered around'.[86] Not a street singer himself, Dati was a priest who composed the text to be performed. Another example of the performative nature of news ballads can be found in the work of Eustachio Celebrino, a picaresque and peripatetic figure,

Significance of Contrafactum in Execution Ballads,' *Past and Present* 229, no. 1 (2015): 47–89.

[81] McIlvenna, *Singing the News of Death*, 60.

[82] Tessa Watt, *Cheap Print and Popular Piety, 1550–1640* (Cambridge: Cambridge University Press, 1991), 64–6; McIlvenna, *Singing the News of Death*, 63–4.

[83] Rebecca Oettinger, *Music as Propaganda in the German Reformation* (Aldershot: Ashgate, 2001), 89–90.

[84] Hyde, *Singing the News*, 86–9; McIlvenna, *Singing the News of Death*, 54.

[85] Salzberg, *Ephemeral City*, 59.

[86] Giuliano Dati, *La storia della inuentione delle nuoue insule di Channaria indiane* (Rome: Eucario Silber, 1493).

educated in medicine and philosophy at Padua, a maker of woodcuts, a gambler, hack writer, and street singer. Opening a poem on the flood that affected the city of Rome in 1523, he writes:

> I come spectators, to announce to you
> - if I may have your courteous silence -
> something never heard before [. . .]
> make sure that there is no shouting or noise,
> for I am an ambassador sent from the heavens [. . .]
> therefore keep silent if you please.[87]

Likewise, a Dutch song which reported on the Sack of Antwerp in 1576 addressed its audience directly: 'What news I will explain to you / Want to hear a sad one?'.[88] *A lamentable new Ballad vpon the Earle of Essex his death* included a refrain and opened by inviting the audience to join in the singing (Figure 5), as can be heard in Audio 1.[89] In fact, the number of songs with refrains suggests that communal singing was commonplace. Sarah Williams suggested that the printers of seventeenth-century English broadside ballads indicated sections for communal singing by visually separating the text through the use of, for example, multiple typefaces.[90]

---

[87] Eustachio Celebrino, *La dechiaratione per che none venuto il diluuio del. M. D. xxiiij* (Venice: for Francesco Bindoni & Mapheo Pasini compagni, c. 1525).

[88] 'De Spaengiaerts Voor Vyanden Verclaert Zijnde Van De Staten, Bedrijven Groote Tyranny Met Rooven, Moor Den, Branden, Vrouwen Schenden Als Geschiet Is Te Maestricit Ende Teantwerpen' ['The Spanish having been declared enemies of the States-General, practise great tyranny with robbery, murder, arson, raping women as has happened in Maastricht and Antwerp'], in *Nieuw Geuʒenlied-Boek*, ed. Hendrik Jan van Lummel (Utrecht: Kemmer, 1871).

[89] *A lamentable new Ballad vpon the Earle of Essex his death* . . . (London: for Cuthbert Wright, 1625).

[90] Sarah Williams, *Damnable Practises: Witches, Dangerous Women, and Music in Seventeenth-Century English Broadside Ballads* (Farnham: Ashgate, 2015), 129.

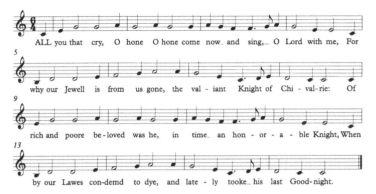

ALL you that cry, O hone O hone come now and sing, O Lord with me, For

why our Jewell is from us gone, the val - iant Knight of Chi - val-rie: Of

rich and poore be-loved was he, in time an hon - or - a - ble Knight, When

by our Lawes con-demd to dye, and late - ly tooke his last Good-night.

Figure 5 *A lamentable new Ballad vpon the Earle of Essex his death to the tune of the Kings last good-night.* London: for Cuthbert Wright, 1625.

Audio 1 Verse 1 of *A lamentable new Ballad vpon the Earle of Essex his death to the tune of the Kings last good-night* sung by Jenni Hyde. Audio file available at www.cambridge.org/communicatingthenews

---

It is arguable that the performative aspects of these works – including intonation, gesture, rhyme, and music – were important to their impact. Communicating news in rhyme and with particular tunes made them easier to memorise, to pass on, or to adapt to later events, but it seems likely that seasoned performers of ballads also exploited tone of voice and gesture in order to capture and keep the audience's attention.

3.4 Actors, Spaces, and Publics

In the aural circulation of news, a key role was played by peripatetic and multi-faceted figures such as street singers or vagrant performers. Street singers were crucial actors in European Renaissance urban and information culture, mediating between printed, written, and oral forms of communication.[91] Performing

---

[91] Luca Degl'Innocenti and Massimo Rospocher, eds., 'Street Singers in Renaissance Europe,' special issue, *Renaissance Studies* 33, no. 1 (2019).

in the central piazzas or on busy street corners, they offered news and commentary on current events to heterogeneous urban publics. The men who sang and sold news songs were usually highly mobile. The English ballad seller Richard Sheale, for instance, had a route that took him from London to Tamworth, in the Midlands, and claimed to be the earl of Derby's retainer.[92] The acclaimed Italian publisher and itinerant performer Jacopo Coppa, originally from Modena, found success in cities as diverse as Naples, Ferrara, Bologna, Rome, Florence, and Venice.[93]

Throughout Europe, however, ballad singers and itinerant sellers were often negatively associated with vagrancy and sometimes criminality. At best, they were seen as unreliable; at worst, they were associated with cutpurses and pickpockets. In Italy and Spain, these figures were often associated with forms of disability that placed them on the margins of society. Lameness and blindness were among the most common. Blind singers in Spain, who were often associated in brotherhoods, specialised in prayers but were also among the successful authors of news songs in the sixteenth and seventeenth centuries.[94] They combined the performative and authorial dimensions; for example, the blind performer Martín de Langa from Calatayud (Zaragoza), who was an author of various *relaciones de sucesos* (reports of events) as well as a professional musician, was often employed by urban authorities.[95]

Though socially marginal, these itinerant figures are ubiquitous in the iconography of early modern Italian cities. They could also sometimes be portrayed in the woodcuts that adorn the printed ballads. Likewise, they are a common feature of early modern genre paintings, appearing in street

[92] Andrew Taylor, *The Songs and Travels of a Tudor Minstrel: Richard Sheale of Tamworth* (York: York Medieval Press, 2012).

[93] Luca Degl'Innocenti and Massimo Rospocher, 'Urban Voices: The Hybrid Figure of the Street Singer in Renaissance Italy,' *Renaissance Studies* 33, no. 1 (2019): 17–41.

[94] Abel Iglesias Castellano, *Entre la voz y el texto: los ciegos oracioneros y papelistas en la España moderna (1500–1836)* (Madrid: Consejo superior de investigaciones, 2022).

[95] Ibid.

scenes, marketplaces, and fairs.[96] But if the purveyors of news ballads were generally men from the lower social orders, this does not necessarily mean that the songs were written by people from this social group. In England and Italy, where we can identify the composers of songs, they tend to be people with some level of education.[97] For the most part, however, ballad writers or performers in England and Italy remained anonymous.

Such entertainers occupied the central public spaces of major European cities. Itinerant ballad sellers deliberately set up their wooden stalls in places where people gathered. They sang their songs in taverns and at fairs, but they were most commonly found in marketplaces, piazzas, bridges, and street corners. These were already spaces where people went to look for information and discuss the news and where official proclamations were read and posted, marking the transition of news and information from private to public. As such, ballad singers drew on the existing authority of these public spaces, exploiting their association with authority and official pronouncements of policy, but they also contributed to an evanescent public sphere because these were sites where diverse publics assembled to hear and discuss the news.[98]

Street singers were a regular presence in the Italian urban soundscape and in the busiest spaces of sociability. They entertained crowds and sold their news ballads in public spaces such as Piazza Navona and Campo de' Fiori in Rome, Piazza San Martino in Florence, Piazza of Porta Ravegnana in Bologna, and Piazza San Marco and the Rialto area in Venice.[99]

---

[96] Chrischinda Henry, 'From Beggar to Virtuoso: The Street Singer in the Netherlandish visual tradition, 1500–1600,' *Renaissance Studies* 33, no. 1 (2018): 136–58. See also Jenni Hyde, 'From Page to People: Ballad Singers as Intermediaries in the Early Modern Graphosphere,' in *Transactions of XI International Conference on the History of Written Culture (CIHCE)* (Gijon: Trea, forthcoming).

[97] Hyde, *Singing the News*, 32–6; Degl'Innocenti and Rospocher, 'Urban Voices.'

[98] Massimo Rospocher and Rosa Salzberg, 'An Evanescent Public Sphere: Voices, Spaces, and Publics in Venice During the Italian Wars,' in *Beyond the Public Sphere: Opinions, Publics, and Spaces in Early Modern Europe*, ed. Massimo Rospocher (Berlin-Bologna: Dunker & Humlot-Il Mulino, 2012), 93–114.

[99] Rosa Salzberg and Massimo Rospocher, 'Street Singers in Italian Renaissance Urban Culture and Communication.' *Cultural and Social History* 9, no. 1 (2012): 9–26.

The centre of the English broadside ballad trade was London, particularly around St Paul's Cathedral where booksellers had their stalls. But broadside ballads were the epitome of cheap print: not made to last but easy to transport from London across the country in the pack of a travelling balladeer or hawker. In eighteenth-century Paris, newsmongers gathered around the tree of Cracow, which stood at the heart of Paris in the gardens of the Palais-Royal, while ragged street singers performed at the Pont Neuf.[100] In early modern Spain, that function was fulfilled by the *mentidores* (meeting or gossiping points), public spaces of information and entertainment 'where idle people met to talk', gossip, and share information.[101] In Madrid, blind singers assembled mainly at the *mentidores* located at the Puerta del Sol, on the corner of Mayor street, at the San Felipe steps, and at the corner of Santa María and León streets; in Seville, the *mentidero* occupied the square in front of the Cathedral;[102] in Valencia, the circulation of prints and news ballads gravitated around the market square.[103]

Media historians have illuminated ballad singers' capacity to act as oral proto-journalists by providing not only entertainment but also information and breaking news to wide publics and heterogeneous audiences. Teodoro Barbieri closed his verse account of the Battle of Marignano with a reference to the sale of the printed text aimed at a socially diverse audience: 'So to the poor man as to the citizen (*cittadino*) / you have the story and I'll keep the penny (*quattrino*)'.[104]

---

[100] Robert Darnton, 'An Early Information Society: News and the Media in Eighteenth-Century Paris,' *American Historical Review* 105, no. 1 (2000): 1–35, here 2–3.

[101] Antonio Castillo Gomez, 'The Alborayque and Other Street Readings in the Early Modern Hispanic World,' in *Kreuz- und Querzüge. Beiträge zu einer literarischen Anthropologie*, ed. Harm-Peer Zimmermann, Peter O. Büttner, and Bernhard Tschofen (Hannover: Wehrhahn Verlag, 2019), 167–89, here 179–80.

[102] Ibid.

[103] Juan Gomis Coloma, *Menudencias de imprenta. Producción y circulación de la literatura popular (Valencia, siglo XVIII)* (Valencia Institució Alfons el Magnànim, 2015).

[104] Teodoro Barbieri, *El fatto darme del christianissimo re di Franza contra Sguizari. Fatto a Meregnano appresso a Milano del MDXV adi XIII de septembre* (Venice c. 1515).

Publics were composed of people belonging to different social classes, as shown by correspondence which offers extraordinary evidence of how Italian news ballads could circulate among diverse audiences and move around the Mediterranean. In August 1510, the Venetian merchant Martino Merlini wrote to his brother, at that time stationed between Beirut and Aleppo. He informed his brother of the latest 'news discussed on the piazzas'. Mixing gossip and official information, the merchant attached to the letter a printed news song about the war between Venice and Ferrara, writing, 'I am sending you a *frottola*-ballad newly printed from Ferrara'. This ballad, he explained, had been performed four days earlier on the public square in Ferrara and then put out for sale, and he assured his brother that he would send others, which he thought would be available by the end of the day.[105] The original print sent to Beirut no longer survives, but a copy of the same ballad is preserved in a collection of popular printed news-songs assembled by Cardinal Ippolito d'Este.[106] A cardinal belonging to one of the most important Renaissance dynasties enjoyed this material for the same reasons as the humble merchants: entertainment and information. He was by no means the only avid collector from high social strata of these ephemeral materials: one only has to think of the immense collection of printed ballads assembled by Hernan Colon, illegitimate son of Christopher Columbus.[107] In England, the self-made man Samuel Pepys was an avid collector of broadside ballads, while the presence of ballad tunes in elite music manuscripts demonstrates their appeal at the highest level.

---

[105] Giuseppe dalla Santa, 'Commerci, vita privata e notizie politiche dei giorni della lega di Cambrai. Da lettere del mercante veneziano Martino Merlini,' *Atti del reale Istituto Veneto di scienze lettere ed arti* 76, part 2 (1916–17): 1548–605, here 1596–7.

[106] Massimo Rospocher, 'News in Verse: The Battle of Polesella (1509) between Imagination, Communication, and Information,' in *Turning Tales: Essays on History and Literature in Honor of Guido Ruggiero*, ed. Mary Lindemann and Deanna Shemek (Newark: University of Delaware Press, forthcoming).

[107] José María Pérez Fernández and Edward Wilson-Lee, *Hernando Colón's New World of Books: Toward a Cartography of Knowledge* (New Haven and London: Yale University Press, 2021).

3.5 Truth and Fiction

Street singers were sometimes considered unreliable and dishonest purveyors of news and information. Yet their news songs proliferated especially around major military events or political controversies – be it the War of the League of Cambrai in Italy, the Exclusion Crisis in England, the Dutch revolt in the Netherlands, or the Reapers War (or Catalan Revolt) that affected the Principality of Catalonia. Reliable or not, their accounts of current events were sought after by listeners and readers. Titles often used 'the lexicon of news'.[108] Street singers advertised both the performance and the selling of their texts by shouting titles and first lines which highlighted their novelty and reliability: *The truthful news of Brescia point by point as it happened*, a ballad announcing the reconquest of Brescia by the Venetians in February 1512, was printed in the lagoon city just a few days after the event.[109] In a news ballad about the military defeat of the Venetian against the French at Agnadello (1509), the anonymous author declares that he had composed and brought it to the printer only two days after the event had taken place.[110] Street singers responded to a 'present' that unfolded rapidly, producing texts intended for immediate consumption. Within a few days, they were able to put an account of a battle to verse, perform it publicly, and sell it.

But if the novelty of news was important, reliability was essential. It was well known that compositions circulated mixing fact and fiction. The author of *The Siege of Padua* declared that in his poetical narrative there was no room for 'Fairies, monsters, serpents, lions, tigers, centaurs, satyrs, giants, princess' or for the adventures of the popular chivalric heroes; but, he promised, 'I shall sing to you about all the bitter and difficult things'.[111] Meanwhile, *A description of a strange (and*

---

[108] Raymond, *Pamphlets and Pamphleteering*, 105.

[109] *La vera nova de Bressa de punto in punto come andata* . . . (Venice: Alessandro Bindoni, c. 1512).

[110] *La miseranda rotta de venetiani a quelli data da lo invictissimo et christianissimo Ludovico re de Franʒa et triumphante duca de Milano* (Milano 1509), f. 4v.

[111] Bartolomeo Cordo, *La obsidione di Padua ne la quale se tractano tutte le cose che sonno occorse dal giorno che per el prestantissimo messere Andrea Gritti proueditore generale fu reacquistata* . . . (Venice 1510), f. 2v.

miraculous) Fish noted that although some would think it 'a lie', his tale was 'certaine true'.[112] The Romagnol friar Giraldo Podio da Lugo derided those gullible customers who, in order to satisfy their thirst for information, threw away their money by acquiring pamphlets containing 'badly-written verses', 'lies', and the fantasy tales of street singers. In contrast, in his *True story of everything that happened in Ravenna* (1512), the cleric guaranteed:

> I deliberated with myself
> That, in order to satisfy everyone,
> I would tell the truth plainly
> Exactly as it happened.[113]

The appetite for news ballads describing the events 'exactly as they happened' was clearly strong. In England, at least twenty-seven ballads were written about the Armada Crisis, which might indicate how ravenous people were for news of the potential invasion.[114] One gave a detailed account of how the English navy managed to defeat one huge ship, the *Galleazzo*, and sank the *Callice*.[115] Much of the information given in the song, set to the tune of 'Monsieur's Almain' (Figure 6) and which can be heard in Audio 2, can be corroborated from other sources. Some English ballads have even been shown to have linguistic similarity with officially sanctioned publications.[116]

[112] Martin Parker, *A description of a strange (and miraculous) Fish* ... (London: for Thomas Lambert, 1635).

[113] Giraldo Podio da Lugo, *Hystoria vera de tutto il seguito a Ravenna* [*s. l.* c. 1512], f. 1r.

[114] John J. McAleer, 'Ballads on the Spanish Armada,' *Texas Studies in English Literature and Language* 4 (1963): 602–12, 602.

[115] Thomas Deloney, *A joyful new Ballad, declaring the happie obtaining of the great Galleazzo* ... (London 1588).

[116] Edward Wilson-Lee, 'The Bull and the Moon: Broadside Ballads and the Public Sphere at the Time of the Northern Rising (1569–70),' *Review of English Studies* 63, no. 259 (2012): 225–42.

This great Gall - eaz - zo, which was_ so huge and hye: That__
like_ a bul -warke on the sea, did seeme to each_ mans eye.
There was it tak - en, un - to_ our great re - liefe: And__
di - vers Nob - les in which traine Don Pie - tro was_ the chiefe.
Stronge__ was she_ stuft, with Can-nons great and small: And
o - ther in - stru - ments of warre, which we ob - tain - ed_ all.
A____ cer - taine signe, of good suc -cesse we trust That
God will o - ver - throw the rest, as_ he hath done the_ first.

Figure 6 Verse 4 of Thomas Deloney, *A joyful new Ballad, declaring the happie obtaining of the great Galleazzo to Monsieur's Almain*. London 1588.

Audio 2 Verse 4 of Thomas Deloney, *A joyful new Ballad, declaring the happie obtaining of the great Galleazzo to Monsieur's Almain* sung by Jenni Hyde. Audio file available at www.cambridge.org/communicatingthenews

Nevertheless, English news ballads occupied a difficult intellectual space. The English parliament held the privilege of free speech, but for everyone else, discussing current affairs could easily verge on sedition. From 1557, all printed materials were supposed to be entered in the Stationers' Company's register, which acted as a form of official oversight.[117] Many English ballads therefore avoided directly addressing matters of high politics, concentrating on less contentious issues such as international affairs or rebellions. At times,

[117] Watt, *Cheap Print*, 43.

balladeers were forced to hide the true meaning of their songs, using a knowing or implicit subtext to comment on contentious matters.[118] By the mid-seventeenth century, some typographical distinctions emerged. Those which required either explanation or pre-existing knowledge were often printed in white-letter type. More accessible songs continued to be produced in black letter.[119] Nevertheless, such visual differences would have had little impact on those who heard them sung.

Sometimes, we know about ballads only because they are mentioned in court records, perhaps because they were libellous or, conversely, came too close to the truth. At times, their content was considered politically or socially threatening. In the politically heated climate of the Italian Wars, the publisher-performer Niccolò 'Zoppino' was arrested in Venice in March 1510, accused of having performed and sold in the piazza of Ferrara a political song against the Venetian State.[120] In 1596, as a second consecutive harvest failed, the English balladeer Thomas Deloney published 'a certein ballad conteyning a complaint of the great want and scarcity of corn w[i]thin this realm'. The genre itself seems to have been a problem. Ballads might move the masses to action. Deloney's words and music came together 'that thearby the poor may aggravate their grief and take occasion of soom discontentment'.[121] Likewise, during the French Wars of Religion, satirical songs attacked religious and political targets. Whilst never being 'brazenly seditious', they formed part of a news culture which engaged the commons with politics.[122] Their interactive components helped to create a feeling of belonging to the Catholic League, part of a whole spectrum of

---

[118] Hyde, *Singing the News*.

[119] Angela McShane, 'Typography Matters: Branding Ballads and Gelding Curates in Stuart England,' in *Book Trade Connections from the Seventeenth to the Twentieth Centuries*, ed. John Hinks and Catherine Armstrong (London: British Library, 2008), 19–44, here 29.

[120] Massimo Rospocher, '"In vituperium Status Veneti": The case of Niccolò Zoppino,' *The Italianist* 34, no. 3 (2014): 349–61.

[121] London, British Library, Lansdowne MS 81, f. 76r.

[122] Kate van Orden, 'Cheap Print and Street Song following the Saint Bartholomew's Massacres of 1572,' in *Music and the Cultures of Print*, ed. Kate van Orden (Abingdon: Routledge, 2017), 271–323, here 272–3.

anti-Royal practices organised by the League which included processions, communal chanting of ballads, and joint attacks on royal coats of arms.[123] During the Italian wars of the first half of the sixteenth century, ballads had a similar function, often reporting the latest news with a propagandistic bent in favour of one of the parties to the conflict. Ballads were therefore something to be feared by the authorities, and governments regularly took steps to control them.

3.6 Emotions and Sensationalism

Although matters of politics featured heavily in popular songs, many ballads sold 'true stories' of crime and punishment. True crime began to feature in European ballads from the sixteenth century. Sensationalistic and moralistic murder ballads were among the most successful editorial and performative genres in sixteenth-century Italy. Murder ballads included those that spoke from the perspective of the victim of the crime or a close relative lamenting the dead. The sixteenth-century lament of a Paduan gentlewoman whose husband murdered her three young daughters, before committing suicide, is a particularly vivid example of this category. The singer adopted the voice of the victim offering bloodthirsty description of the murder of the three innocent young daughters (their throats slit with a razor), and of the mother's discovery of their violated bodies, in order to provoke a strong emotional response in the audience.[124] Some ballads included laments in the voice of the condemned criminal, a Europe-wide phenomenon in the early modern period; in others, an omniscient narrator recounted the events.[125]

---

[123] Alexandra Schäfer-Griebel, *Die Medialität der Französischen Religionskriege. Frankreich und das Heilige Römische Reich 1589* (Stuttgart: Beiträge zur Kommunikationsgeschichte, 30, 2018), 102 and 366.

[124] *Lamento d'vna gentildonna padouana che'l suo marito ammazzò tre loro picciole figliuole, et poi se stesso, questo istesso anno MDLII* (Venice [1552]).

[125] Rosa Salzberg and Massimo Rospocher, 'Murder Ballads: Singing, Hearing, Writing and Reading about Murder in Renaissance Italy,' in *Murder in Renaissance Italy*, ed. Trevor Dean and Kate Lowe (Cambridge: Cambridge University Press, 2017), 164–88.

I Am a poore prison-er con-dem-ned to dye, ah woe is me woe is me for my great fol-ly, Fast fet-tred in y-rons in place where I lie Be war-ned young wan-tons,hemp passeth green hol-ly My par-ents were of good de-gree by whom I would not coun-selled be, Lord Je-su for-give me with mer-cy re-leeve me, Re-ceive O sweet sav-iour my spirit un-to thee.

Figure 7 *Luke Huttons lamentation … To the [t]une of Wandering and wavering* ('Welladay'). London 1598.

One popular sub-genre of crime ballad was the 'goodnight'. These were songs ostensibly written by criminals the night before their execution. *Luke Huttons lamentation* warned its listeners not to commit the same sins as the supposedly eponymous anti-hero.[126] Hutton's three-year career as a highwayman came to an end when he was captured and faced 197 indictments at York assizes. The scansion of the lines and placement of the refrains suggest that the tune was almost certainly 'Welladay' (Figure 7), which can be heard in Audio 3. It maximised the potential for audience participation by including a refrain and two repeated lines. Suitably repentant before his death, Hutton recommended that his friends (and, by extension, his audience) imagine what it was like to be him: 'Thinke on my words when I am gone'. These attributes have a paradoxical effect: although the songs represented 'punishing state power as a shaper of

---

[126] *Luke Huttons lamentation …* (London 1598).

subjective experience', they also 'enabled a vicarious participation in deviant lives'.[127]

Audio 3 Verse 1 of *Luke Huttons lamentation . . . To the [t]une of Wandering and wavering* ('Welladay') sung by Jenni Hyde. Audio file available at www .cambridge.org/communicatingthenews

---

But there was also a wider interest in extraordinary stories, as the 'news world of the sixteenth and seventeenth centuries was full of portents'.[128] News ballads of natural disasters (earthquakes, fires, or floods), monstrous births, epidemics and plagues, miracles, wonders of the New World, miraculous healings, and heinous crimes circulated throughout Europe, so much so that it seems to be at the dawn of the phenomenon of 'sensationalism'. Like news pamphlets, sixteenth-century ballads never missed an opportunity to press home a moral or religious lesson. In the second half of the sixteenth century, in post-Tridentine Italy, news ballads served increasingly as an effective means of moral indoctrination. Indeed, Tessa Watt revealed a similar significant trend towards the production of 'godly' ballads in late sixteenth-century England.[129] This process of combining specific details about an event with more general moral and religious warnings was common in news ballads across Europe. This godly or moralising content can be seen as a form of editorial, providing a framework through which the audience heard and understood the news.

Joy Wiltenburg notes that 'sensationalist text uses emotional resonance to draw its audience, assuming a given emotional response' in order to shape 'shared values and individual identity'.[130] She suggests that 'emphasis on familial relationships, graphic descriptions of violence, and the inclusion of direct dialogue worked along with emotive language to enhance visceral

---

[127] Joy Wiltenberg, 'Ballads and the Emotional Life of Crime,' in *Ballads and Broadsides in Britain, 1500–1800*, ed. Patricia Fumerton, Anita Guerrini, and Kris McAbee (Farnham: Ashgate, 2010), 173–86, here 174.

[128] Pettegree, *The Invention of News*, 252.

[129] Watt, *Cheap Print*.

[130] Joy Wiltenburg, 'True Crime: The Origins of Modern Sensationalism,' *American Historical Review* 109, no. 5 (2004): 1379–80.

effect'.[131] As well as stressing their newsworthiness, news ballads emphasised the 'lamentable', 'horrible', or 'pitiful' nature of the tale. An English ballad, *Anne Wallens Lamentation*, was set to the common execution ballad tune, 'Fortune My Foe'.[132] The first part contained the moralising first-person account of Wallen's repentance and God's judgement on her crime but was topped with the image of Mistress Wallen stabbing her husband with a chisel. His head is turned away, while his hands are open, palms facing his wife, in a gesture of shock more than self-defence. The second part is illustrated with an image of a woman being burned at the stake while crowds look on, but the tone shifts dramatically, recording the gruesome details of Mistress Wallen's unprovoked attack. Infuriated by his patient bearing of her tirade of abuse, Wallen confesses that 'Amongst his intrailes I this Chissell threw, / Where as his Caule came out', allowing his intestines to spill from his body. She then recounted her husband's words of horror: 'What hast thou don, I prethee looke quoth he, / Thou hast thy wish, for thou hast killed me' (Figure 8). This can be heard in Audio 4. Sensationalist language was replicated across Europe. Norwegian skilling songs also regularly had titles such as *The Unfortunate Incident*, *The cruel murder*, or *The terrible conflagration*.[133]

Audio 4 Verse 15 of T. Platte, *Anne Wallens Lamentation* to 'Fortune My Foe' sung by Jenni Hyde. Audio file available at www.cambridge.org/communicatingthenews

Sensationalist ballads called for emphatic reactions from the audience. Their emotionally charged content brought into the cultural mainstream news of 'deviant actions' that would in reality be on the very edges of people's experience.[134] They depended on emotive qualities to shape a common response in their audience. While this was common to prose pamphlets as well as ballads, how much more emotive might a song be with the addition of music? Performance, and especially music, increased access

[131] Wiltenburg, 'True Crime,' 1382–3.
[132] T. Platte, *Anne Wallens Lamentation* . . . (London 1616).
[133] Brandtzæg, *Skillingsvisene i Norge*, 101.
[134] Wiltenburg, 'True Crime,' 1377–8.

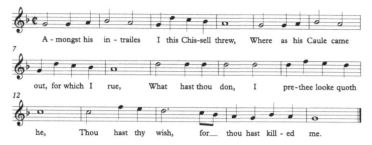

Figure 8 Verse 15 of T. Platte, *Anne Wallens Lamentation* to 'Fortune My Foe'. London 1616.

to the text and helped to shape the responses of a group wider than just those who could read the printed text. Moreover, music creates physical and emotional responses in both performer and audience.[135] If the emotional appeals of early sensationalist texts, such as direct speech, emotive language, and religious resonance, were a 'key rhetorical device' rather than cheap, thrill-seeking entertainment, then ballads amplified this effect through their music.[136]

3.7 Conclusion

Despite differences in their material form and the time period in which they became popular, news ballads across Europe shared many significant features. They were performed in urban public spaces by itinerant performers who often encouraged audience participation in the form of communal singing and relied on the emotional engagement of their listeners. The music to which the songs were set was easy to learn, and it helped to spread the message not only through its mnemonic features but also, at times, through added layers of meaning. The news these songs purveyed, about crime, war, rebellion, politics, and providence, might sometimes have

---

[135] William Forde Thompson, *Music, Thought and Feeling: Understanding the Psychology of Music* (Oxford: Oxford University Press, 2009), 124–57.

[136] Wiltenburg, 'True Crime,' 1397.

lacked detail, but the social context of performance created a space for the discussion of current affairs. Occasionally, this spilled over into sedition, even though the majority of songs emphasised the social norms and moral implications of transgression.

While the role of ballads in spreading the news remains complex, in early modern Europe, it is clear that topical songs emphasised their newsworthiness and the accuracy of the stories they told. Ballads were predicated on a social culture in which information was spread by word of mouth, and therefore the amount of information in a ballad was not a direct indicator of its function in news culture. Their intermediality, combining information with entertaining performance in public spaces, was the key to their success. It helped to create a sense of community, brought about a collective response to news of disaster, crime, and rebellion, and spoke to a wide range of social groups. Far from being mere titillation or propagandist moralising, these songs created an emotional resonance which brought people together in shared understandings of news or a chance to ponder the nature of religious and political power.

4 News Counts

4.1 Introduction

The study of news has been greatly impacted by the digital revolution: we now mostly access news sources through digital surrogates and, increasingly, harvest the resulting data to study patterns, language, and news flows on a large scale. What, then, do computational methods bring to the study of early modern news? In this section, we survey existing computational approaches, and through a case study we suggest that one impact of these new methods is the possibility of looking past national or linguistic barriers. The section aims to show that computational methods have the potential to break the 'nation-state bias' now prevalent in media studies and go some way to dispel the myth of a straightforward boundary between 'early modern' and 'modern' periodicals. When a data-driven, international picture is taken into account, the history of the news form is not as straightforward as a progression from *newsbook* to *newspaper*.

In this section, we take into account the developments in the digital humanities as they apply to news. The current digital and computational approaches to news are sketched out. We argue that the basis of news, the paragraph, is particularly important when we consider computational approaches. Through a comparative case study, of London in 1649 and Helsinki in 1820, we analyse the news as it appears through geographic and relational data and consider the extent to which a computational approach breaks down some of the temporal and geographic barriers that appear when news is studied primarily through material forms.

While the 'digital turn' in the humanities has put a fresh emphasis on the quantifiable aspects of texts, news has long been framed in terms of measurements and quantities. In his play *The Staple of Newes*, first performed in 1625, Ben Jonson satirised news as something which could be manufactured and traded like any other commodity. Implicit in this assessment of news is that it is also something measurable – that it could be enumerated and registered in a merchant's ledger alongside any other stock for sale. As Cymbal (the manager of the news agency, or 'staple' in the play) puts it when praising one of his clerks: 'A decay'd stationer/He was, but knows news well, can sort and rank 'em.'[137]

This view of a 'good' way to approach news is echoed in the views of historians and bibliographers of the twentieth century. The first projects to catalogue newsbooks systematically had an inherently quantitative nature. Folke Dahl, who undertook one of the first projects to create a bibliography of early modern newsbooks at an issue level, wrote that '[. . .] when the newspaper historian had "sorted [all extant copies of newspapers] typologically and arranged them in series [. . .] he has in the main completed his work."'[138]

This tendency to 'sort and rank' news can be traced to some of its distinct textual properties. As will be outlined in section 4.4, the most important 'unit' of early modern news was not a single text, article, or issue but rather the paragraph: generally a collection of all the news dispatched from a particular place, headed with a place and date. News in this form has some inherent structured, quantitative properties: it centres dates, places, and other discrete, quantifiable, and consistent pieces of information, and one can quite easily build structured databases of the quantitative aspects of news. Of course, other texts do have structured information: books contain imprints listing authors, publishers, and places, not to mention internal structures such as chapters, sections, and paragraphs. But early modern news has a different kind of consistent, internal structure: paragraphs of news can be compared across texts and languages; they can be 'sorted and ranked' in a way that chapters in a book, for example, cannot. They contain information standardised across a number of languages and cultures: entities such as places, people, and dates (with some important caveats). News, we argue, is therefore uniquely suited amongst historical texts to the methods of quantitative analysis.

---

[137] Ben Jonson, *The Staple of News* (first performed 1625[6]; first published in 1631).

[138] Folke Dahl, *Amsterdam Earliest Newspaper Centre of Western Europe: New Contributions to the History of the First Dutch and French Corantos* (Dordrecht: Springer Netherlands, 1939), 11–12.

4.2 News in Early Modern and Modern Europe

From the sixteenth century onwards, the press became an integral part of European and global communication and functioned as an instrument of modernisation.[139] During its centuries-long history, the newspaper has varied a great deal as a cultural and material object. The late nineteenth-century paper, comprising seven or even eight columns per page, was a very different artefact from the first printed news sheets that often had only one column. The differences are not only temporal but also local since news-papers were published under varied conditions, with an array of technolo-gies. Newspaper history, rather than being a linear narrative, is characterised by an uneven development, by breaks and ruptures, and by different temporal rhythms.

4.2.1 The *Moderate Intelligencer*

During the early 1600s, the production and dissemination of news were often inconsistent, and various partnerships and syndicates published irre-gular and sometimes unreliable content.[140] The first English news publica-tion was a small folio sheet produced in Amsterdam in 1620, followed by news printed in London with false Amsterdam imprints.[141] In 1621, London-based news publications with genuine London imprints emerged,

---

[139] Raymond and Moxham, *News Networks*, 5–11; Jürgen Osterhammel, *The Transformation of the World: A Global History of the Nineteenth Century* (Princeton, NJ: Princeton University Press, 2014), 712–23.

[140] See Jayne E. E. Boys, *London's News Press and the Thirty Years War*, Studies in Early Modern Cultural, Political and Social History, vol. 12 (Woodbridge: Boydell Press, 2011); Joad Raymond, *The Invention of the Newspaper: English Newsbooks, 1641–1649* (Oxford: Oxford University Press, 1996); Joseph George Muddiman, *A History of English Journalism: To the Foundation of The Gazette* (London: Longmans, 1908); Michael Frearson, 'London Corantos in the 1620s,' *Studies in Newspaper and Periodical History* 1, no. 1–2 (January 1993): 3–17; Joseph Frank, *The Beginnings of the English Newspaper, 1620–1660* (Cambridge, MA: Harvard University Press, 1961).

[141] Folke Dahl, *A Bibliography of English Corantos and Periodical Newsbooks 1620–1642* (Stockholm: Almquist och Wiksell, 1953); Laurence Hanson, *English Newsbooks: 1620–1641* (London: Bibliographical Society, 1938), 358.

and these continued until 1632 when a decree from the Star Chamber banned all printed news until 1638. When production resumed, the corantos were replaced by parliamentary diurnals, which were produced without central control from 1641 to 1649.[142] During this time, readers in London had access to a range of news titles, including our subject, the *Moderate Intelligencer*, which was known for its high-quality foreign news and long run from 1645 to 1649. This newsbook was published by John Dillingham – a successful tailor but by then an experienced editor – and ran to 239 issues in total.[143] The title was printed first by Robert White and then, following a dispute and an attempted takeover, by Robert Leybourne. Despite a missing issue and the occasional counterfeit imitator, it stands out as a consistent title in an inconsistent landscape. Only Samuel Pecke's *Perfect Diurnall* clearly bested it in terms of length of run, reputation, and reliability of publication. Joseph Frank, though dismissive of the title because of its perceived blandness, remarked that its very longevity meant that by the end of its run it was amongst the better-quality titles of the period.[144]

4.2.2 Finlands Allmänna Tidning

Finlands Allmänna Tidning emerged in 1820 in a quite different historical setting. Newspaper publishing had flourished in London already for centuries, but in the region that became known as Finland, newspapers gained a foothold rather slowly. Finland had been part of the Swedish Kingdom for centuries. In Sweden, newspaper publishing had started in 1645 when the first issue of *Ordinari Post Tijdender* appeared. Its purpose was to deliver information from abroad at the time of the Thirty Years War. Soon, it was also regarded as important to write on domestic affairs, and letters to the editors were sent via the postal networks. Still, the real growth of the press in Sweden was realised in the 1750s and 1760s. During this wave, in 1771,

---

[142] Raymond, *Invention*, 12.

[143] Anthony N. B. Cotton, 'John Dillingham, Journalist of the Middle Group,' *The English Historical Review* 93, no. 369 (1978): 817–34, here 818; Joad Raymond, 'Dillingham, John (fl. 1639–1649), Journalist,' in *Oxford Dictionary of National Biography* (Oxford: Oxford University Press, 2004).

[144] Frank, *Beginnings*, 187.

Tidningar Utgifne af et Sällskap i Åbo, by Henrik Gabriel Porthan and other academics, was published in the city of Turku, in the south-western corner of Finland. This is regarded as the first Finnish newspaper. The one printing house in the city was tailored for academic dissertations and therefore the format of the paper became similar to a book. In subsequent decades, newspapers were published only in Turku, which was the administrative, academic, and religious centre of the region. At the turn of the century, everything changed. After the 1808–1809 war between Sweden and Russia, Finland was detached from Sweden and annexed to the Russian Empire. It became a Grand Duchy under Russian rule which lasted until Finnish Independence in 1917. The political changes were not favourable for publishing activities, and during the first decades of the nineteenth century, the media landscape remained basically the same. Until 1820, papers were published only in Turku, and print runs were very limited. After Helsinki became the capital of the Grand Duchy, it was natural to launch a newspaper there too, and *Finlands Allmänna Tidning* was established. Soon, papers also appeared in Vyborg, initially in German (*Wiburgs Mancherley*, 1821, and *Wiburgs Wochenblatt*, 1823). The fourth newspaper city was Oulu, where *Oulu Wiikko-Sanomia* started in 1829. In 1820, however, besides *Finlands Allmänna Tidning*, only two papers appeared in the country: *Åbo Tidningar* and *Turun Wiikko-Sanomat* in Turku; the first was published in Swedish, the latter in Finnish. Under these circumstances, it is evident that there could not be any intensive circulation of news within Finland, but news was copied or translated directly from foreign papers.[145]

News from abroad was one of the main strands of what *Finlands Allmänna Tidning* was supposed to publish. In the process, the printing of foreign news was kept under control. The Russian Empire had tightened its hold over media after the French Revolution and the Napoleonic Wars. It

---

[145] Päiviö Tommila, 'Yhdestä lehdestä sanomalehdistöksi 1809–1859' (From one newspaper into a press, 1809–1859, in Finnish), *Suomen lehdistön historia. Sanomalehdistön vaiheet vuoteen 1905* (Kuopio: Kustannuskiila, 1988), 175–8; Hannu Salmi, Asko Nivala, Heli Rantala, Reetta Sippola, Aleksi Vesanto, and Filip Ginter, 'Återanvändningen av text i den finska tidningspressen 1771–1853,' *Historisk tidskrift för Finland* 103, no. 1 (2018): 46–63.

was important to take care that no subversive or revolutionary content circulated. The press was significantly shaped by censorship, but the year 1820 was still quite liberal. Press control became much sharper during the reign of Nicholas I (1825–55). The censorship decree enacted in 1829 was the basis of speech control until the freedom of the press decree of 1865.[146]

4.3 Digital Methods

Recent years have seen a growth in harnessing digital methods to understand early modern historical datasets, such as using text analysis to look at the Early English Books Online (EEBO) and Eighteenth Century Collections Online (ECCO) collections. This ranges from using text analysis techniques to digitally 'read' many texts and look at changes in linguistic concepts[147] to quantifying changes in print culture through library catalogue metadata.[148] Although the generally accepted beginning of computational approaches to text can be traced to the work done by Roberto Busa to index the works of Thomas Aquinas on IBM punch cards, carried out between 1946 and 1976, quantitative work on news texts was slow to start.[149] The few projects which did look at news texts aimed to use news to understand more about the communication infrastructure, in a manner similar to the analysis of postal speed times to understand European

---

[146] On censorship conditions in Finland, see Tommila, 'Yhdestä lehdestä sanomalehdistöksi 1809–1859,' 102–5.

[147] For example, Peter De Bolla, *The Architecture of Concepts: The Historical Formation of Human Rights* (New York: Fordham University Press, 2013); Peter De Bolla, Ewan Jones, Paul Nulty, Gabriel Recchia, and John Regan, 'Distributional Concept Analysis,' *Contributions to the History of Concepts* 14, no. 1 (2019): 66–92.

[148] Leo Lahti, Niko Ilomäki, and Mikko Tolonen, 'A Quantitative Study of History in the English Short-Title Catalogue (ESTC), 1470–1800,' *LIBER Quarterly* 25, no. 2 (4 December 2015): 87–116; Leo Lahti, Jani Marjanen, Hege Roivainen, and Mikko Tolonen, 'Bibliographic Data Science and the History of the Book (c. 1500–1800),' *Cataloging & Classification Quarterly* 57, no. 1 (2019): 5–23.

[149] Steven E. Jones, *Roberto Busa, S. J., and the Emergence of Humanities Computing: The Priest and the Punched Cards* (New York: Routledge, 2016), 1–26; Hannu Salmi, *What is Digital History?* (Cambridge: Polity, 2021), 6.

communication.[150] A key example here is Paul Ries's 1977 article 'The Anatomy of a Seventeenth-century Newspaper', which used quantitative methods to study the differences in transmission speeds of news from four newspapers in 1669. Later research on news counted datelines to understand the 'backbone' of the news network in Europe[151] or look at it from a corpus linguistics and sociolinguistics perspective.[152] However, in the early days, news text was not made available or analysed for style or linguistics in the same way as other text datasets. This is despite the fact that news, perhaps more than most historical objects of study, is suited to quantitative research.

This dearth of quantitative newspaper research has changed in the last twenty years. Bob Nicholson's 2013 article asked whether we were then on the cusp of a 'digital turn' in media history.[153] It is no coincidence that Nicholson's area of expertise is the Victorian press: most data-driven research into English-language news history has focused on the nineteenth and twentieth centuries, in part at least because of the large amount of text data available, thanks to a greater output, numerous digitisation projects, and the use of Optical Character Recognition (OCR). This data, totaling millions of pages of print, has been used to investigate aspects of nineteenth-century disease, poverty, crime, and industrialisation.[154] More relevant recent work on nineteenth-century news has looked at text re-use. The 'Viral Texts' project and its follow-up, 'Oceanic Exchanges', sought to understand the spread of news by

---

[150] See, for example, Fernand Braudel, *The Mediterranean and the Mediterranean World in the Age of Philip II* (London: Collins, 1972), 187; Wolfgang Behringer, 'Communications Revolutions: A Historiographical Concept,' *German History* 24, no. 3 (2006): 345.

[151] Paul Arblaster, 'Posts, Newsletters, Newspapers: England in a European System of Communications,' *Media History* 11, no. 1–2 (2005): 21–36.

[152] Nicholas Brownlees, *The Language of Periodical News in Seventeenth-Century England* (Newcastle upon Tyne: Cambridge Scholars Pub, 2011).

[153] Bob Nicholson, 'The Digital Turn: Exploring the Methodological Possibilities of Digital Newspaper Archives,' *Media History* 19, no. 1 (2013): 59–73.

[154] On recent projects on newspaper history, see, for example, Estelle Bunout, Maud Ehrmann, and Frédéric Clavert, eds., *Digitised Newspapers – A New Eldorado for Historians? Reflections on Tools, Methods and Epistemology* (Berlin: De Gruyter Oldenbourg, 2023).

detecting clusters of re-used passages.[155] Recent projects have used digital humanities techniques to trace concepts and news flows.[156] This is also true of historiographical or methodological surveys of news history: there are important studies of the impact of digitisation on media history, for example, but their main focus is on Victorian or twentieth-century periodicals.[157]

Despite the huge attention given to quantitative studies of later news as well as the inherent structural and quantitative properties of it as outlined above, the computational study of *early modern* news is still in its infancy. Two notable databases of early modern news collected news from the *Paris Gazette* and the Fugger newsletter collection, respectively.[158]

[155] See Ryan Cordell, 'The Viral Texts Project,' accessed 6 January 2023, http://viraltexts.github.io/; Ryan Cordell, 'Oceanic Exchanges,' accessed 6 January 2023, http://oceanicexchanges.github.io/.

[156] Adán Israel Lerma Mayer, Ximena Gutierrez-Vasques, Ernesto Priani Saiso, and Hannu Salmi, 'Underlying Sentiments in 1867: A Study of News Flows on the Execution of Emperor Maximilian I of Mexico in Digitized Newspaper Corpora,' *Digital Humanities Quarterly* 16, no. 4 (2022); Jaap Verheul, Hannu Salmi, Martin Riedl, Asko Nivala, Lorella Viola, Jana Keck, and Emily Bell, 'Using Word Vector Models to Trace Conceptual Change over Time and Space in Historical Newspapers, 1840–1914,' *Digital Humanities Quarterly* 16, no. 2 2022); Jana Keck, Mila Oiva, and Paul Fyfe, 'Lajos Kossuth and the Transnational News: A Computational and Multilingual Approach to Digitized Newspaper Collections,' *Media History* (2022): 1–18.

[157] James Mussell, 'Elemental Forms: The Newspaper as Popular Genre in the Nineteenth Century,' *Media History* 20, no. 1 (2014): 4–20; James Mussell, *The Nineteenth-Century Press in the Digital Age* (New York: Palgrave Macmillan, 2012); Paul Fyfe, 'An Archaeology of Victorian Newspapers,' *Victorian Periodicals Review* 49, no. 4 (2016): 546–77; Maria DiCenzo, 'Remediating the Past: Doing "Periodical Studies" in the Digital Era,' *English Studies in Canada* 41, no. 1 (2015): 19–39.

[158] See Nikolaus Schobesberger, 'Mapping the Fuggerzeitungen: The Geographical Issues of an Information Network,' in *News Networks in Early Modern Europe*, ed. Joad Raymond and Noah Moxham (Leiden: Brill, 2016); Stéphane Haffemeyer, 'Public and Secret Networks of News: The Declaration of War of the Turks against the Empire in 1683,' in *News Networks in Early Modern Europe*, ed. Joad Raymond and Noah Moxham (Leiden: Brill, 2016), 805–23.

The metadata of the paragraphs on place and dates of printing is a valuable source which allows researchers to measure the circulation of news throughout Europe because of this standardised format. In both cases, the information was used to produce statistical analyses and visualisations. One of the few projects that used (what at the time were) state-of-the-art approaches was by Giovanni Collavizza *et al.*, who used text re-use detection methods to understand flows in early modern Italian news.[159] With the exceptions of projects such as these, studies looking at news in this way have been relatively rare, in part because there is no metadata standard for doing so. The sparse structure of news metadata helps to represent this multitude of perspectives: when news is broken into its individual parts and represented as numerical and geographic values, some of the differences across the centuries dissolve. While the form of the newspaper changed considerably, the basic unit, the paragraph, remained static for much longer.

The long-term development of the press has been studied in numerous national press histories[160] and comprehensive histories of communication.[161] In recent decades, more and more transnational histories and projects have

---

[159] Giovanni Colavizza, Mario Infelise, and Frédéric Kaplan, 'Mapping the Early Modern News Flow: An Enquiry by Robust Text Reuse Detection,' in *Social Informatics, Lecture Notes in Computer Science*, ed. Luca Maria Aiello and Daniel McFarland (Cham: Springer International Publishing, 2015), 244–53.

[160] Margot Lindemann, *Deutsche Presse bis 1815. Geschichte der deutschen Presse Teil I* (Berlin: Colloquium Verlag, 1969); Kurt Koszyk, *Deutsche Presse im 19. Jahrhundert. Geschichte der deutschen Presse* (Berlin: Colloquium Verlag, 1966); Rudolf Stöber, *Deutsche Pressegeschichte: Von den Anfängen bis zur Gegenwart*, 3rd ed. (Köln: Herbert von Halem Verlag, 2014); *Suomen lehdistön historia. Sanomalehdistön vaiheet vuoteen 1905* (Kuopio: Kustannuskiila, 1988).

[161] Marshall T. Poe, *A History of Communications: Media and Society from the Evolution of Speech to the Internet* (Cambridge: Cambridge University Press, 2010); Jukka Kortti, *Media in History: An Introduction to the Meanings and Transformations of Communication over Time* (London: Red Globe Press, 2019).

focused on the transfer of information across borders.[162] In the history of communication, however, early modern and modern newspapers are seldom studied in conjunction. The aim of this section is to bring together two – perhaps unexpected – points of comparison: an English paper, the *Moderate Intelligencer*, published in London in 1649 and a Finnish paper, *Finlands Allmänna Tidning*, published in Helsinki in 1820. We are interested in their similarities and differences, particularly in how they conveyed information from the rest of the world to their readers. Their historical context was different, but on the other hand, the setting helps to elucidate the haphazardness, or asymmetry, of newspaper history. To put it another way, do data science and quantitative analysis serve to illuminate or obscure the diachronic changes in news across Europe? Did European news in this period have enough shared points of connection to allow meaningful general conclusions to be made?

4.4 The Paragraph as Unit of News

Key to this is the idea of comparable news units. As outlined in the first section, 'News Moves', the central format of news in early modern Europe was the news paragraph. The basic unit of news was not a single article or story but a short block of text, usually with a dateline, which contained all the news sent from a particular place. It has been shown that these paragraphs circulated semi-independently and were copied, translated, and put into news publications when needed.[163] Newspapers in the seventeenth century were composite in that they contained a variety of reports of

---

[162] For example, 'Oceanic Exchanges: Tracing Global Information Networks in Historical Newspaper Repositories, 1840–1914,' https://oceanicexchanges .org/; The European dimensions of popular print culture (EDPOP), https:// edpop.wp.hum.uu.nl/; Joad Raymond and Noah Moxham, eds., *News Networks in Early Modern Europe* (Leiden and Boston: Brill, 2016).

[163] Slauter, 'Paragraph as Information Technology,' 253–78; Brendan Dooley, 'International News Flows in the Seventeenth Century: Problems and Prospects,' in *News Networks in Early Modern Europe*, ed. Joad Raymond and Noah Moxham (Leiden; Brill, 2016), 175.

most events; the aim was to allow the reader to interpret the flow of the narrative rather than just the final story. Sometimes this meant multiple, contradictory versions of the same story from different sources in the same title. Newspapers were collaborative in that they involved a wide and ever-changing range of actors, including newsletter writers, printers, editors, and translators, and they were iterative in that they changed, updated, and retold stories over time as new details or sources emerged. Studies of early modern news which seek to use a data-driven approach should take this into account.

The features of early modern newsbooks were still visible in 1820 (Figures 9 and 10). The news paragraph had remained as the basic unit of information. In Finland, foreign news items were copied from papers from, for example, London, Paris, Stockholm, and St. Petersburg. Most news items were still short, seldom longer than a paragraph, although during the course of the nineteenth century, longer and more journalistic articles on foreign affairs became increasingly published. From the 1840s onwards, a new form of news was introduced, the telegramme, which again stressed the role of the paragraph in news delivery. In the 1860s, the transatlantic cable, and soon other transcontinental connections, enabled the quick exchange of messages.

4.4.1 Comparative Study of the *Moderate Intelligencer* and *Finlands Allmänna Tidning*

This comparative study relies on two datasets of structured news meta-data with very different temporal and geographic properties: first, a dataset of metadata information for the news paragraphs from the *Moderate Intelligencer* for all issues in the year 1649 and, second, a dataset of metadata on the news paragraphs published in *Finlands Allmänna Tidning*, Helsinki, including all issues from the year 1820. The layout of these titles is key to understanding how they can be compared. The layout of the *Moderate Intelligencer*'s foreign news was rather systematic and was generally inserted as a block with its own, separate chronological structure, nested within the week's domestic news. There is a recognisable micro-structure to the paragraph. Each paragraph contained, in a separate line of text, the place of dispatch,

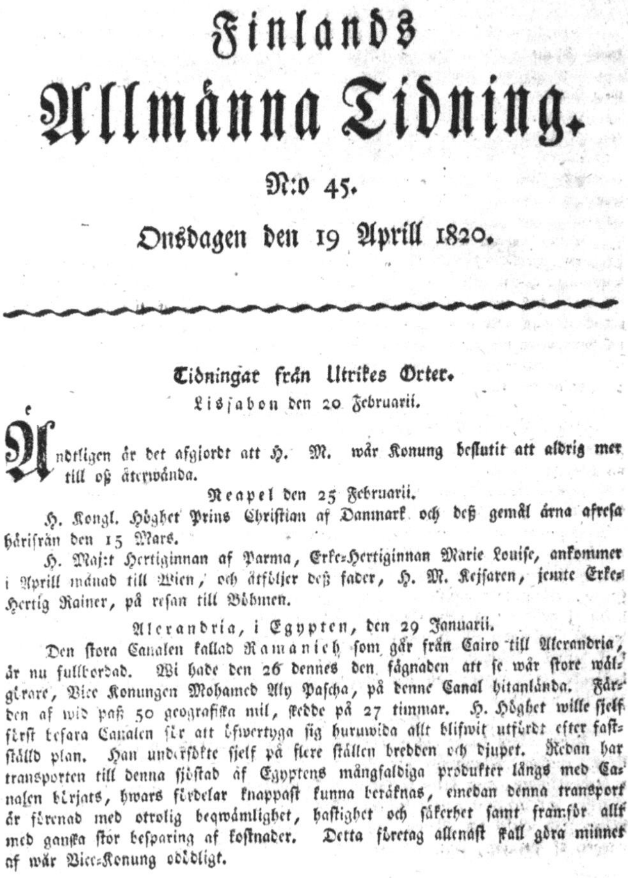

Finlands

Allmänna Tidning.

N:o 45.

Onsdagen den 19 April 1820.

Tidningar från Utrikes Orter.

Lissabon den 20 Februarii.

Ändtligen är det afgjordt att H. M. wår Konung beslutit att aldrig mer till oß återwända.

Neapel den 25 Februarii.

H. Kongl. Höghet Prins Christian af Danmark och deß gemål ärna afresa härifrån den 15 Mars.

H. Maj:t Hertiginnan af Parma, Erke-Hertiginnan Marie Louise, ankommer i April månad till Wien, och åtföljer deß fader, H. M. Kejsaren, jemte Erke-Hertig Rainer, på resan till Böhmen.

Alexandria, i Egypten, den 29 Januarii.

Den stora Canalen kallad Ramanieh som går från Cairo till Alexandria, är nu fullbordad. Wi hade den 26 dennes den fägnaden att se wår store wälgörare, Vice Konungen Mohamed Aly Pascha, på denne Canal hitanlända. Färden af wid paß 50 geografiska mil, skedde på 27 timmar. H. Höghet wille sjelf först besara Canalen för att öfwertyga sig huruwida allt blifwit utfördt efter fast-ställd plan. Han undersökte sjelf på flere ställen bredden och djupet. Redan har transporten till denna sjöstad af Egyptens mångfaldiga produkter längs med Ca-nalen börjats, hwars fördelar knappast kunna beräknas, emedan denna transport är förenad med otrolig beqwämlighet, hastighet och säkerhet samt framför allt med ganska stor besparing af kostnader. Detta företag allenäst skall göra minnet af wår Vice-Konung odödligt.

Figure 9 Front page of *Finlands Allmänna Tidning*, showing the title, the number, the date (Wednesday, 19 April 1820), and paragraphs of foreign news. Image from the Digital Collection of the National Library of Finland. https://digi.kansalliskirjasto.fi. Public domain.

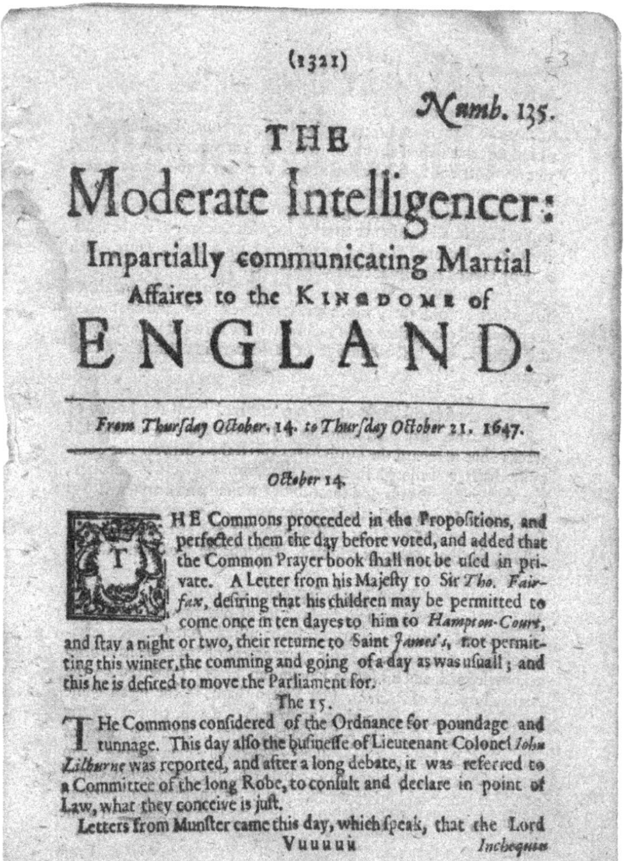

(1321)

Numb. 135.

THE
Moderate Intelligencer:

Impartially communicating Martial
Affaires to the KINGDOME of

ENGLAND.

From Thursday October. 14. *to Thursday October* 21. 1647.

October 14.

THE Commons proceeded in the Propositions, and
perfected them the day before voted, and added that
the Common Prayer book shall not be used in private. A Letter from his Majesty to Sir Tho. Fair-
fax, desiring that his children may be permitted to
come once in ten dayes to him to Hampton-Court,
and stay a night or two, their returne to Saint James's, not permit-
ting this winter, the comming and going of a day as was usuall; and
this he is desired to move the Parliament for.

The 15.

THe Commons considered of the Ordnance for poundage and
tunnage. This day also the businesse of Lieutenant Colonel John
Lilburne was reported, and after a long debate, it was referred to
a Committee of the long Robe, to consult and declare in point of
Law, what they conceive is just.

Letters from Munster came this day, which speak, that the Lord
Vuuuuu   Inchequin

Figure 10 Front page of *Moderate Intelligencer*, showing title, numbering, and paragraphs of domestic news. John Dillingham. *The moderate intelligencer: impartially communicating martiall affaires to the kingdome of England* (London, Robert White: 1647), Call #: M2324.6 no. 135. Used by permission of the Folger Shakespeare Library under a Creative Commons Attribution-ShareAlike 4.0 International License.

nearly always a date of dispatch, and then within the paragraph there is sometimes further information, firstly about where the news has been relayed from, followed by the location or origin of the news story itself. The paragraphs were likely written by local news correspondents and professional news scribes in the town or city mentioned in the dateline. They probably arrived in London publications from Paris before being translated; evidence for this is that there exist two translations of the same texts, in titles published in the same week.[164]

The result from this collection was metadata for 871 and 380 paragraphs of foreign news in the *Moderate Intelligencer* and *Finlands Allmänna Tidning*, respectively, across 94 and 83 locations. When possible, we noted down 'secondary' locations of news – for example, if a paragraph was headed Venice but within this was some variation of 'from Constantinople we hear', Constantinople was named as a secondary point of dispatch. This resulted in 151 and 17 secondary places of dispatch. The data was collected manually by reading the digitised images of each issue and recording all the metadata for each paragraph of news, including the place and date on the headline as well as the date it was published. This was then linked to geographic information, from which it was possible to make a series of statistical comparisons and visual maps.

Comparison of these two sources shows notable differences (Figure 11 and Figure 12). In general, there were fewer locations in 1820 overall, and hubs or centres for news circulation have become more pronounced; news was more concentrated in a smaller number of cities. Both show a spread of news throughout Europe, whereas only the Finnish title has significant paragraphs from outside the continent. In 1649 in England, the Low Countries were a very important source of news; this was not the case in Finland in 1820. This perhaps reflects a mixture of England's very close ties (geographically and politically) to the Netherlands and also the diminishing role that the Dutch Republic had in world affairs by 1820. A similar case is Venice, which declined significantly in importance in the intervening time

---

[164] For evidence and discussion of this, see Laurent Curelly, *An Anatomy of an English Radical Newspaper: The Moderate (1648–9)* (Newcastle upon Tyne: Cambridge Scholars Publishing, 2017), 105.

Figure 11 Count of the origins of news paragraphs, *Moderate Intelligencer*, January 1649–October 1649. Data collected by hand from all extant copies, access through Early English Books Online.

but was a very prominent city in 1649. On the other hand, 1649 saw little news from Spain, but by 1820, from the perspective of Finnish papers, Madrid was a key source of news paragraphs. Despite some regional differences in the two cases (Helsinki has slightly more news from Northern European cities, and London in 1649 slightly more from the Low Countries), a similar backbone of European news hubs can be seen: Paris, Italian cities, cities of the Holy Roman Empire, and the Low Countries. This suggests that the news sources looked surprisingly similar even from two very different parts of Europe.

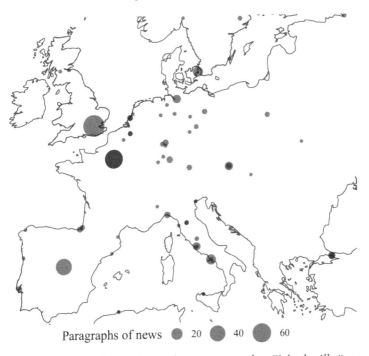

Paragraphs of news   ● 20   ● 40   ● 60

Figure 12 Count of the origins of news paragraphs, *Finlands Allmänna Tidning*, January 1820–December 1820. Data collected by hand from all published issues, access through the digital collection of the National Library of Finland.

4.4.2 Secondary Locations

Through the secondary locations, we find what we might term 'relay locations': places through which news is passed on its route to the final destination. The secondary points tended to be peripheral but still influential locations within the network: Dublin, for example, was usually the relay point for Irish news on its way to London via Chester. Places on the way to the edges of Europe, Eastern European and Mediterranean towns or coastal cities along the Adriatic Sea, tended to be used as secondary relay points for news from further afield. By counting these secondary points, we can construct an even more detailed picture than the 'spine' of news communications available from counting datelines. Some local patterns are visible. There were clusters of relay points surrounding some of the key primary locations: Paris, Venice, and Dublin. Other cities served as both primary and secondary points, including The Hague, Madrid, Hamburg, Vienna, Münster, and Warsaw (Figure 13). These places tended to be on the edges

Paragraphs of news   ● 2   ● 4   ● 6   ● 8

Figure 13 Secondary points of dispatch, *Moderate Intelligencer*, January–October 1649. Secondary points of dispatch are those mentioned within paragraphs (e.g. 'by way of Candia we hear . . .'). Data collected manually by the authors.

in a Europe-wide perspective, geographically peripheral or coastal, but very much at the centre of regional communication networks.

The role of the secondary locations is key to understanding the flow of news. The analysis shows that these secondary cities, generally more peripheral, were crucial in bringing news back to the centre. These were often cities close to but not directly involved in main news events. Mapping the first and secondary points gives a number of patterns. Primary points of dispatch, being the final relay points before the place of publication, tended to be further west and close to the spine of the main postal routes travelling through Europe's centre. Secondary places tended to be further east and often along coasts: news was sent or dispatched from cities all along the coasts of the Italian peninsula and the Adriatic Sea.

4.4.3 Globalisation of News

The biggest quantitative difference we see between the two titles is the increased globalisation of the news by 1820 (Figure 14). From the point of view of transport technology, there is not much difference between the way news could be disseminated in 1649 and 1820. It is obvious that in 1820 news reached Helsinki and Finland in the same way as had happened in previous decades and centuries. It was only after the 1820s, when steamship services began to transform maritime connections, that a major change in transport took place. Later, railways and telegraph lines changed the situation even further. What is clear, however, is that the historical context had changed. The press played an important role in the construction of civil society, and news events, above all political news, had an increasing impact.

The American War of Independence in 1776, and the events that led up to it, put the transatlantic world firmly in the news spotlight. The transatlantic link was reinforced by the fact that the struggle for American independence inspired the French Revolution in 1789. In turn, events in North America and France shook political life everywhere, not only in Europe but also in Latin America, where aspirations towards independence were fuelled. The Napoleonic Wars weakened the colonial hold of Spain, and several countries in Latin America embarked on the independence struggle in the 1810s. In Mexico, Miguel Hidalgo declared the country independent in September 1810, leading to

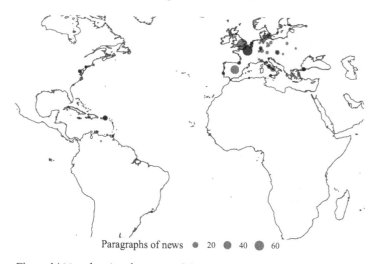

Paragraphs of news ● 20 ● 40 ● 60

Figure 14 Map showing the extent of the news locations in *Finlands Allmänna Tidning*, 1820. A comparable map of the *Moderate Intelligencer* is not shown, as it had almost no news sent from outside Europe.

a war that ran through the decade. Colombia declared independence in 1813. This was confirmed in 1819 when Simón Bolívar defeated the Spanish forces at Boyacá. Chile, on the other hand, declared itself independent after a long battle on 12 February 1818.[165]

The events in the New World generated widespread interest in Europe. There were not only political but also economic reasons to follow these upheavals. The Napoleonic Wars, for example, made it difficult to import sugar from Latin America to Europe. In 1820, the *Finlands Allmänna Tidning* broke the barriers of Europe with its news coverage and regularly followed what was happening on the other side of the Atlantic. In this sense, news was globalised, even if the focus was mainly on the West. In 1820,

[165] Jay Kinsbruner, *Independence in Spanish America: Civil Wars, Revolutions, and Underdevelopment* (Albuquerque: University of New Mexico Press, 2000), xxii, 123.

there was almost no news from Asia and Africa, but Latin America appeared regularly in the press in Finland. News paragraphs named places such as Curaçao, Jamaica, Trinidad, and Venezuela as well as Buenos Aires, Montevideo, and Rio de Janeiro. Even St. Thomas in the West Indies and Angostura in Colombia appear as first locations.

The visibility of Latin America can also be interpreted in the light of political culture in early nineteenth-century Finland. In 1809, Finland had been annexed to the Russian Empire after a century-long period as a province of the Swedish Kingdom. In 1820, *Finlands Allmänna Tidning* was particularly keen to follow not only Latin American struggles for independence but also Southern Italian revolts.[166] Finland, which was still in the process of being assimilated into an empire, was particularly interested in following political movements and growing radicalism. In this sense, the globalisation of news had internal, social, and cultural ramifications. The period of rather liberal news mobility ended soon, however. In 1825, when Nicholas I became Emperor of Russia, control of the press tightened, leading to decades of censorship of international news. The French revolutions of 1830 and 1848 in particular led the regime to tighten its grip on the media.

4.4.4 Temporalities of News Publishing

News movements can be analysed not only spatially but also temporally. Time and space are intertwined, and spatial change is always a temporal process. The further the news travels, the older the information it conveys. If viewed from a single geographical point, the world seems to be constructed from different temporal spheres. The closer the information has come, the more recent it has been. For centuries, the flow of news followed similar pathways and was shaped by similar conditions. Postal routes, trade connections, and shipping and road networks were the platforms along which the news travelled. The speed of news coverage remained quite similar from the mid-seventeenth to the early nineteenth centuries.

---

[166] Hannu Salmi, Jukka Sarjala, and Heli Rantala, 'Embryonic Modernity: Infectious Dynamics in Early Nineteenth-Century Finnish Culture,' *International Journal for History, Culture and Modernity* 8, no. 2 (2020): 114–16.

Everything changed, however, when the telegraph accelerated the flow of information from the 1830s onwards.

However, the flow of information was not linear, let alone smooth or symmetrical. The speed at which news travelled was influenced by political conditions, including how secure the established routes were. The rhythm of news delivery was also influenced by the borders between states and empires and the problems of crossing them. Mobility was furthermore related to the cycle of the seasons. In the Baltic Sea, for example, the winter made it very difficult for mail to get through.

4.5.1 Temporality in *Finlands Allmänna Tidning*

Digitised newspaper collections allow the temporal nature of news transmission to be examined on a larger scale. The metadata of newspapers contains publication dates, from which the frequency of publication can be viewed. Of course, the publication dates can also be found in newspaper issues themselves, but a digital press corpus allows the publication data to be processed as a large dataset. The content of news items, on the other hand, most often included the date on which the information was transmitted. Figure 15 shows a news paragraph in the 7 January 1820 issue of *Finlands Allmänna Tidning*.

The origin of the news is given as Constantinople, and the date as 26 October 1819. It remains unclear exactly by which routes the news was transmitted and how many intermediaries, and newspapers, there were in

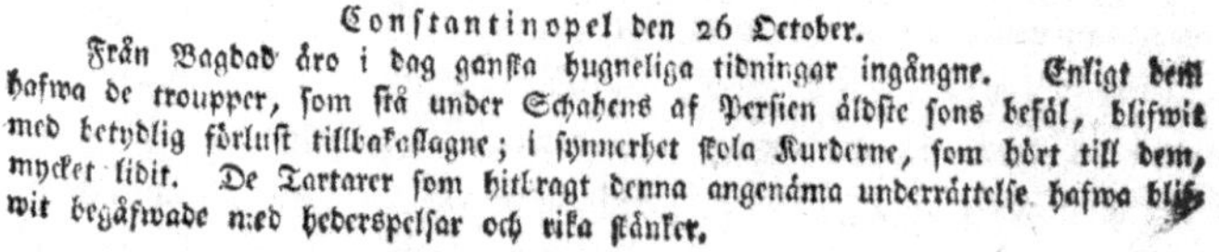

Tidningar från Utrikes Orter.

Constantinopel den 26 October.

Från Bagdad äro i dag ganska hugneliga tidningar ingångne. Enligt dem hafwa de troupper, som stå under Schahens af Persien äldste sons befäl, blifwit med betydlig förlust tillbakaslagne; i synnerhet skola Kurderne, som hört till dem, mycket lidit. De Tartarer som hitbragt denna angenäma underrättelse hafwa blifwit begåfwade med hedersspelsar och rika skänker.

Figure 15 A news paragraph from *Finlands Allmänna Tidning*, 7 January 1820. Image from the Digital Collections of the National Library of Finland. https://digi.kansalliskirjasto.fi. Public domain.

between. The reader of the newspaper could observe from the timescale how long the news had been in circulation. In this case, these dates gave a delay of 73 days. In the same year, the newspaper published ten other news items with Constantinople as their place of origin. If all the news items for the year were counted, the average time for a news item to travel from Constantinople to Helsinki was 66 days. The longest journey took 86 days in the winter months of 1819–1820, the shortest only 49 days in the autumn of 1820.

For a clearer picture of the seasonal variation, it is possible to consider the news that arrived from London to Helsinki in 1820. There were 77 news items marked as being from London during the year. Of these, 20 were published in June and July 1820, and the news had started their journey in May and June. Figure 16 shows the average transit times, in days, by date of departure.

As the figure shows, the average transit time was under 30 days in April, May, June, July, and August. Seasonal variation appears in two ways: the delivery of news was more fluent but at the same time was more abundant.

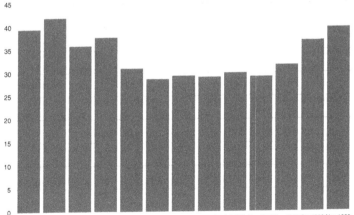

Figure 16 Delivery times of news from London to Helsinki published in *Finlands Allmänna Tidning* in 1820 (y = days, x = the month of transmission).

Recently, the research project *Information Flows across the Baltic Sea: Swedish-language press as a cultural mediator, 1771–1918* concentrated on the study of text re-use. The project was based on a computational method that can detect textual repetition. After 7.5 million pages of digitised newspaper corpora from the National Libraries of Sweden and Finland were combined, it was possible to locate 21.9 million cases of reprinting, limited to all passages of text that were over 300 characters and appeared at least twice in the material.[167] These findings consist of various kinds of content, but they included news items that were copied from Sweden to Finland, or vice versa. In fact, 80 per cent of cross-border re-use chains originated from Swedish papers which were important providers, and mediators, of foreign news for Finnish papers. In 1820, the traffic was still small-scale because there were only a few newspapers in Finland. The database of text re-use, which is open access at textreuse.sls.fi, includes 488 texts that have travelled between Finland and Sweden.

This material sheds light on some of the news that was published in *Finland Allmänna Tidning* in 1820. One example is the news from Curaçao, dated 16 May 1819. The text deals with Venezuela, which had separated from Spain in 1811 and become independent. The news suggests that Venezuela will return under the Spanish regime. The news was published in *Stockholmsposten* in Sweden on 17 July 1820 and reprinted in *Finlands Allmänna Tidning* on 24 July, one week later. Obviously, the news had been translated into Swedish for *Stockholmsposten* and then copied to Finland, word for word. The British Library Newspapers database shows that in early July similar news on Venezuela, via Curaçao, were published in several papers, such as *Trewman's Exeter Flying Post* (6 July 1820) and *Royal Cornwall Gazette* (8 July 1820). These papers indicate that the rumours on Venezuelan incidents had in fact been delivered through the Dutch press. Indeed, the newspaper *Opregte Haarlemsche Courant* in Haarlem had told of these developments

---

[167] Patrik Lundell, Hannu Salmi, Erik Edoff, Jani Marjanen, Heli Rantala, eds., *Information Flows across the Baltic Sea: Towards a Computational Approach to Media History*. Lund: Media History Archives, 2023. DOI:10.54292/s6au8axqht

on 27 June.[168] Obviously, it took over a month for the news to travel across the Atlantic, and thereafter it took several weeks for the story to continue towards the North.

These examples of information flows are processes that took several months to unfold and that can be followed by browsing journals, scrolling through microfilms, or consulting digitised collections. The study of the copying of texts becomes more problematic if the aim is to identify long-term circulation. This broader movement of texts can be discerned only using computer-assisted methods. In the project *Information Flows across the Baltic Sea*, the longest re-use cases were almost as long as the investigated timeframe. In Sweden, texts from the very first papers in 1645 were republished in the late nineteenth century.[169] These were not news, of course, but texts from the past that were activated for present circumstances. Old newspapers became an archive that could be employed in the editorial work during the era of the expansion of the press.

4.5.2 Temporality in the *Moderate Intelligencer*, 1649

Similar patterns can be seen in the *Moderate Intelligencer*. Reliably periodical news was possible only with a reliable and periodic postal system. By 1649, post travelled quickly through the main arterial routes of Britain and Europe. The spread of the manuscript *avvisi* newsletters and thereafter the printed periodical was dependent on the 'development of accessible postal services'.[170] In the British case, in 1635, Charles I issued a proclamation establishing the Public Letter Office in England and Scotland. Letters cost 2d. up to 80 miles, 4d. between 80 and 140 miles, and 6d. above 140 miles.[171]

---

168 *Opregte Haarlemsche Courant*, 27 June 1820, available at the Delpher database at the National Library of the Netherlands, https://resolver.kb.nl/resolve?urn=ddd:010518705:mpeg21:p001.

169 Cluster 11280940, https://textreuse.sls.fi/cluster/search?fq=[%22cluster_id:cluster_11280940%22], accessed 20 December 2022.

170 Schobesberger, 'Fuggerzeitungen,' 19.

171 Mark Brayshay, *Land Travel and Communications in Tudor and Stuart England: Achieving a Joined-up Realm* (Liverpool: Liverpool University Press, 2014), 323.

Mainland Europe's postal system was well developed and available to the public by 1649. The Imperial Post had routes from Brussels across the Alps to Italy, also connecting to Antwerp. Italy, Britain, and later Spain and Portugal all had internal postal systems established by the middle of the seventeenth century. This European postal system had a 'backbone' route running across the continent, with smaller services connecting to it from there, also in a hub-and-spoke formation, albeit with the difference that in this case the hubs were connected in a linear formation. The post, and therefore news, could move relatively quickly through this spine-like system.

With similar metadata to the Finnish case, we can calculate the average age of stories and give an approximation of the age of news from most important European cities. Generally, news from Paris was between six and eight days old by the time it was printed in London; eleven from much of the Netherlands; fifteen from Lyon, Derry, and Cork; between twenty and twenty-five from Frankfurt; twenty-five from Venice and Vienna; and thirty-five to forty days old from Lisbon and Warsaw.

This news was also seasonal. For example, an item of news marked Barcelona sent on 11 December 1646 was published in the *Moderate Intelligencer* on 21 January 1647, a difference of forty-one days; a story from the same city sent on 12 June 1647 was published on 8 July, a difference of twenty-six days.[172] We cannot provide a direct comparison to the news travel times from London to Helsinki in 1649 (Helsinki was a small administrative city in the seventeenth century, and there are no news stories in the *Moderate Intelligencer* headed from there), but examples of other cities display the same pattern of seasonality, as in the example of Rome in Figure 17. Although the overall travel times seem lower, a similar pattern of seasonality can be seen, though not as pronounced as the Helsinki–London route, which was reliant on a sea often frozen in winter.

---

[172] *Moderate Intelligencer* 98, 14–21 January 1647, 59:E.371[16]; *Moderate Intelligencer* 121, 1–8 July 1647, 63:E.397[12].

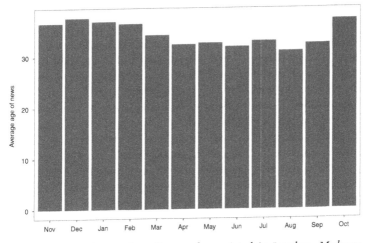

Figure 17 Age of news from Rome when printed in London, *Moderate Intelligencer*. Data collected by the author.

4.5 Conclusions

The previous two sections also dealt with breaking news down into units, either ballads which could be traced or news stories which moved across borders. Digitisation brought with it the promise of transnational research, allowing us to move beyond the 'nation-state bias' inherent in a discipline in which most of its practitioners worked in the archives of a single country. In fact, much computational research has continued to be along national lines, even in the era of the digital. This approach, centring not the text but rather its other constituent parts or units, may help us to finally reach the transnational promise of the digital age.

Techniques such as linguistic analysis, geographic mapping, and network analysis are becoming typical tools of the media or news historian. However, in order for these techniques to be more widely adopted, better metadata standards need to be developed and adopted, and these standards need to take into account this peculiar aspect of early modern news, its division into units, each from a particular place and time. Some work in this area has been done to 'map' existing metadata: one conclusion we can draw from this map is that metadata standards are mostly based around the issue as the basic unit and are more suited to later, article-based, nineteenth- and twentieth-century news.[173] In the case of Britain, most periodical news has been excluded from efforts to OCR or transcribe early modern texts, and the OCR results from early Finnish newspapers in 'fraktur' font are still unsatisfactory. Another problem is that newspapers have often been digitised page by page, and the basic units of the text, such as news paragraphs, might have been broken into two parts, which makes them difficult to identify automatically. The study of news paragraphs, and the development of metadata that would make the study of these paragraphs easier, needs computer-based segmentation tools that can connect broken paragraphs. Having text and metadata that are more accurate would allow us to more fully understand and measure the flows and re-uses of early modern texts. With new tools to do this across languages, we could greatly improve our knowledge of how news worked.

While we might look at the infrastructure and technological and logistical advancements between 1649 and 1820 as impressive, when we look at everyday communication of news in real terms, which is accessible through news metadata, we can see that the changes were not so drastic as one would imagine. Tools are now available which could allow us to extract this information at scale and across different languages, using natural language processings and large language models. Doing so will mean we can more accurately trace the flow of news and information across Europe and show that it is a story of temporal and geographic continuities rather than breaks.

The latest generation of text analysis using artificial intelligence brings with it the promise of matching and retrieving text on the basis of semantic similarities rather than keywords or phrases. This will make a computational

---

[173] Melodee H. Beals and Emily Bell, with contributions by Ryan Cordell, Paul Fyfe, Isabel Galina Russell, Tessa Hauswedell, Clemens Neudecker, Julianne Nyhan, Mila Oiva, Sebastian Padó, Miriam Peña Pimentel, Lara Rose, Hannu Salmi, Melissa Terras, and Lorella Viola, *The Atlas of Digitised Newspapers and Metadata: Reports from Oceanic Exchanges*. Loughborough, 2020. DOI: 10.6084/m9.figshare.11560059.

approach to news even more important as we look even further beyond individual texts and analyse the events themselves. Our aim with the above case study was to show that even with limited semantic information about the places of dispatch, news texts have much to tell us about the general flow of information across Europe. There are limitations in our approach, to be sure. It is obvious that the study of news flows can be, and should be, enriched through the study of actual news texts. In addition to primary and secondary locations, these texts describe foreign events in words and sentences and attach meanings to issues that are far away from the reader. Our aim was, however, to try to demonstrate the value of metadata and, drawing on metadata, to show that large-scale comparisons can be realised on a transnational basis. It follows, therefore, that metadata should be central to our study of news, along with language and their various material forms.

5 Conclusion: Future News History

In this volume, we have sketched out some directions towards which we believe the study of early modern news to be moving. News, as we have shown, travelled across national boundaries and material formats, and although this presents challenges to research, we are beginning to recognise the value of studying transnationally and across genres. However, there is still much more work to be done to understand the connectedness of early modern news cultures. Work is still needed not only to break down international barriers further but also to challenge siloed approaches to news formats. There is work to be done, for example, on the overlap between news ballads and other forms of news media, such as proclamations or pamphlets. Collaboration is needed not just between scholars from different countries but between those working with different textual genres and across different disciplines – from history to geography, to data science – in order to generate a fuller understanding of the complex interrelationships of news cultures in early modern Europe.

And where to stop? Does the system we uncover reflect the datasets we give ourselves? News did not end in the Holy Roman Empire: but do our sources, limited by the reach of archives and libraries and catalogues and language skills, wrongly encourage us to consider that Europe has an edge, that communication runs out? How do we decide what counts as a periphery?

A new perspective on news forms is a start: If the focus is on small parts of a written or printed news publication that are taken up and re-used in other media, a fuller picture of the connectedness and connectiveness of media and regions can be outlined. This new perspective will help to overcome the still-dominating concentration on national frameworks and on news forms – concerning the source material – and bring together researchers from different countries, disciplines, and fields when it comes to research organisation. By doing so, we could finally achieve a joined-up understanding of international news, combining multiple perspectives from the Holy Roman Empire to Finland, from literary history to art historical approaches, and from the postal system to reading practices. Thus, we could approach news as the complex system it clearly was.

The work we have done here is the product of just such an international collaboration, bringing together multiple perspectives, including the joint efforts to access multiple archives, to combine focuses of researchers working on vocals, images, sounds, texts, and data. This kind of collaboration can be fully achieved only with a transformation in the concept and accessibility of news archives. Today, we have better and more thorough sources and metadata standards, and data is much more easily available. The barrier of connecting news in different languages is disappearing; the newest computational methods are by their nature multi-lingual. When they can be fully implemented, it will be possible to truly connect archives, news sources, and news forms. The use of Linked Open Data, a system for sharing data across any number of repositories through the use of common identifiers, will make it much easier for researchers to connect different sources and different forms.

In addition to geographical boundaries, the future will bring greater opportunities to overcome temporal distances. Newspaper collections have been digitised since the 1990s, and hundreds of millions of pages of material are available globally. This is also true for other forms of news media: nowadays, there are also a growing number of digital resources that make it possible to reconstruct the soundscapes of the news in the early modern period. In the 'News Counts' section, we looked at a London newspaper from 1649 and a Helsinki newspaper from 1820 side by side. Our idea was that there are not only differences but also interesting similarities between early modern and modern news reporting. In the future, the extensive newspaper databases will allow for long-term studies that can outline the changing role of the press and the routes of information flow over time.

Better accessibility supports more comparative and comprehensive works: the access to written and even more printed news has become much easier in the last years, but only rarely do researchers know about the collections and databases which are not part of their field of research. The completion of the English Broadside Ballad Archive, for example, has created a freely accessible digital copy and transcription of every extant broadside ballad published in England during the seventeenth century.[174] As other ballad digitisation

---

[174] Patricia Fumerton, dir., *English Broadside Ballad Archive* (http://ebba.english .ucsb.edu) (accessed 8 March 2023).

projects across Europe follow suit, comparative approaches to early modern news ballads will become much more possible, but only if researchers are aware of the work being undertaken in other countries. Comparisons between news forms of different countries could be much easier if there existed more all-encompassing works which linked collections to the overarching databases, blogs, and websites of projects as well as to tools for network analysis and linguistic analysis, for example. Moreover, to make these resources accessible to scholars of all backgrounds, they need to be available in open access.

We might soon be able to reconstruct and understand how people throughout Europe learned about the atrocity of the murder of Henry III in 1589 – whether in the Empire or Italy, the Dutch Republic or England, whether sung or written, played or engraved, whether from news publications moving across borders as a whole or in news-elements, whether available in archives or in digitised collections, whether researchable in Linked Open Data or not – once we embrace the writing of the history of news as a joint venture.

Bibliography

Manuscripts

London: British Library, Add MS 4902.

London: British Library, Lansdowne MS 81.

Wien: Österreichische Nationalbibliothek, Codex 8961–8962 (1588–1589) – Relationes sive novellae quae dicuntur Fuggerianae sermonibus, Germanico, Italico, Gallico etc. conscriptae et ex omni parte Augustam Vindelicorum clarissimis Fuggeris missae. (1568–1605). http://anno.onb.ac.at/cgi-content/anno?aid=fug (2 March 2023).

Printed Sources

A. D. R. L. *Histoire abregee de la vie de Henry de Valois* . . .. Paris: Pierre Mercier, [1589]; woodcut. In Pierre de L'Estoile, ed., *Les belles Figures et Drolleries de la Ligue* . . .. [Paris] 1589–1606 – http://gallica.bnf.fr/ark:/12148/bpt6k859264h (1 March 2023).

Admirable et prodigievse mort de Henry de Valoys . . .. Paris: Pierre Des Hayes, 1589 – Paris: BNF, 8-H-6367 (1).

A lamentable new Ballad vpon the Earle of Essex his death to the tune of the Kings last good-night. London: for Cuthbert Wright, 1625.

Année 1589. Autre Histoire de Jacques Clément . . . s. l. s. d. – Paris: BNF, Qb1, Histoire de France 1589–1610, Sign. M 87884–87899.

Aŭszlegŭng Vnd bedeŭtŭng hierin stehender ʒiefren findet man Klärlich im Trŭck Königliche Declaration intitŭliret. s. l. 1589; etching – Paris: BNF, RES. QB-201 (9)-FOL <p. 9>.

Barbieri, Teodoro. *El fatto darme del christianissimo re di Franʒa contra Sguiʒari. Fatto a Meregnano appresso a Milano del MDXV adi XIII de septembre.* Venice c. 1515.

Bighgnol. *Li horrendi e magnanimi fatti de l'ilustrissimo Alfonso duca di Ferrara contra l'armata de venetiani in Po del mile e cinque cento e noue del mese de decembro a giorni uintidoi.* Ferrara: Baldassare Selli, 1510.

Celebrino, Eustachio. *La dechiaratione per che none venuto il diluuio del. M. D. xxiiij.* Venice: for Francesco Bindoni & Mapheo Pasini compagni, [c. 1525].

Chappell, William. *Popular Music of the Olden Time.* 2 vols. London: Cramer, Beale and Chappell, 1855.

Cordo, Bartolomeo. *La obsidione di Padua ne la quale se tractano tutte le cose che sonno occorse dal giorno che per el prestantissimo messere Andrea Gritti proueditore generale fu reacquistata . . .* Venice 1510.

Dati, Giuliano. *La storia della inuentione delle nuoue insule di Channaria indiane.* Roma: Eucario Silber, 1493.

Deloney, Thomas. *A joyful new Ballad, declaring the happie obtaining of the great Galleazzo, Wherein Don Pietro de Valdez Was the chiefe, through the mightie power and providence of God, being a speciall token of his gracious and fatherly goodnes towards vs, to the great encouragement of all those that willingly fight in the defence of his gospel and our good Queene of England. To the tune of mounseurs Almaigne.* London 1588.

'De Spaengiaerts Voor Vyanden Verclaert Zijnde Van De Staten, Bedrijven Groote Tyranny Met Rooven, Moor Den, Branden, Vrouwen Schenden Als Geschiet Is Te Maestricit Ende Teantwerpen'. In *Nieuw Geuzenlied-Boek*, edited by Hendrik Jan van Lummel. Utrecht: Kemmer, 1871.

Dillingham, John. *Moderate Intelligencer* 98, 14–21 January 1647, E.371[16].

Dillingham, John. *Moderate Intelligencer* 121, 1–8 July 1647, E.397[12].

Dohna, Fabian von. *Die Selbstbiographie des Burggrafen Fabian zu Dohna (1550–1621) nebst Aktenstücken zur Geschichte der Sukzession der Kurfürsten von Brandenburg in Preussen aus dem fürstlich dohnaischen*

Hausarchive zu Schlobitten, edited by Christian Krollmann. Leipzig: Duncker & Humblot, 1905.

Dorne, John. 'The Daily Ledger of John Dorne, 1520.' In *Collectanea*, First Series, edited by F. Madan, 71–178. Oxford: Oxford Historical Society at the Clarendon Press, 1885.

Drey Warhafftige newe Zeitung. Aus Franckreich . . . . Basel: Samuel Apiarius, 1589 – Wien: ÖNB, 20.T.521/Sigel: Alt Prunk.

[Du Mornay, Philippe]. *Declaration dv Roy de Navarre . . . . s. l.* 1589 – Paris: BNF, 8-LB34-733 (A).

El sanguinolento & incendioso assedio del gran turcho contra el christianissimo Rodo. Con epistola del gran turcho a Rodi: et de epsi al gran turcho responsiua in latino prosa tersissima. Venice [c. 1526].

F. Iaqves Clement. s. l. [1589]; engraving. In Pierre de L'Estoile, ed., *Les belles Figures et Drolleries de la Ligue . . . .* [Paris] 1589–1606, f. 16r (below, on the right) – http://gallica.bnf.fr/ark:/12148/bpt6k859264h (1 March 2023).

F. Iaqves Clement. s. l. [1589]; woodcut. In Pierre de L'Estoile, ed., *Les belles Figures et Drolleries de la Ligue . . . .* [Paris] 1589–1606, f. 16r (below, on the left) – http://gallica.bnf.fr/ark:/12148/bpt6k859264h (1 March 2023).

Figure de l'admirable & diuine resolution de F. Iacques Clement . . . . Paris: Roland Guérard / Nicolas Prévost, [1589]; engraving – Paris: BNF, Qb1, Histoire de France 1589–1610, M 87839.

Henry of France. *Indvciae. Frid vnd Anstand . . . .* Frankfurt: Martin Lechler (printer), Pauli Brachfeld (editor), 1589 – Munich: BSB, Res/4 Eur. 345,38.

Henry of France and Henry of Navarre. *Warhaffte vnd eigentliche Beschreibung/ dern Historia . . . .* Colonge: Nikolaus Schreiber, 1589 – Halle: ULB, an Nm 302 (9).

Henry of France and *Parlement* of Paris. *Königliche Declaration Erzehlung . . . .* Straßburg: Bernhard Jobin?, 1589 – Berlin: StaBi, Flugschr. 1588/7A.

Henry of Navarre, Jacques de Ségur-Pardaillan, and Fabian von Dohna et al. *Erklärung/Auß was Vrsachen . . . . s. l.* 1587 – Munich: BSB, Gall.g. 1024 y.

Henry III of France. *Declaration dv Roy svr la trefve . . . .* Tours: Jamet Mettayer, 1589 – Paris: BNF, NUMM-101073 (= Lyon: BM, FC192-22).

Henry III of France. *EDIT DV ROY . . . .* Metz: Abraham Faber, 1589 – Paris: BNF, F-46889 (2).

Henry III of France and Henry of Navarre. *Außschreiben Kön: Mayestat inn Franckreich . . . .* [Straßburg: Bernhard Jobin, 1589] – Munich: BSB, Gall. g. 1023 k.

Kölderer, Georg. *Beschreibunng vnd Kurtze Vertzaichnis Fürnemer Lob vnnd gedenckhwürdiger Historien. Eine Chronik der Stadt Augsburg der Jahre 1576 bis 1607*, vol. 3: 1589–1593 (Codex S 43), edited by Wolfgang E. J. Weber with Silvia Strodel. Augsburg: Wißner-Verlag, 2013.

La miseranda rotta de venetiani a quelli data da lo invictissimo et christianissimo Ludovico re de Franza et triumphante duca de Milano. Milano 1509.

La vera nova de Bressa de punto in punto come andata . . . Venice: Alessandro Bindoni, c. 1512.

Lamento d'vna gentildonna padouana che'l suo marito ammazzò tre loro picciole figliuole, et poi se stesso, questo istesso anno MDLII. Venice [1552].

Le portraict de frere Iacques Clement . . . . [Paris]: Antoine Du Brueil, [1589]; woodcut – Paris: BNF, RES. QB-201 (9)-FOL.

Luke Huttons lamentation: which he wrote the day before his death, being condemned to be hanged at Yorke this last assises for his robberies and trespasses committed. To the /t/une of Wandering and wavering. London 1598.

New Zeytung Auß Franckreich . . . . Cologne: Gottfried von Kempen, 1589 – Bern: UB, ZB Bong V 252:6.

Newe Zeitung aus Franckreich. s. l. 1589 – Berlin: StaBi, Flugschr. 1588/6.

Parker, Martin. *A description of a strange (and miraculous) Fish, cast upon the sands in the meads, in the Hundred of Worwell, in the County Palatine of*

Chester, (or Chesshiere. The certainty whereof is here related concerning the said most monstrous Fish. To the tune of Bragandary. London: for Thomas Lambert, 1635.

[Pinselet, Charles]. *Le Martyre de Frere Iacqves Clement*. Paris: Robert Le Fizelier, 1589 – Paris: BNF, 8-LB34-815.

Platte, T. *Anne Wallens Lamentation, For the Murthering of her husband John Wallen a Turner in Cow-lane neere Smithfield; done by his owne wife, on satterday the 22 of June. 1616. who was burnt in Smithfield the first of July following*. London 1616.

Podio da Lugo, Giraldo. *Hystoria vera de tutto il seguito a Ravenna. s. l.* [c. 1512].

Simpson, Claude. *The British Broadside Ballad and its Music*. New Brunswick: Rutgers University Press, 1966.

[Skinner, John]. *A true relation of the unjust, cruell, and barbarous proceedings against the English at Amboyna*. London: H[umphrey] Lownes (printer), Nathanael Newberry (editor), 1624 – Washington, DC: Folger Shakespeare Library, STC 7451 Copy 1; Digital Image Files 165078 and 64236.

Ware conrafaiung Brueder Iacob Clements . . . . s. l. [1589]; engraving – Paris: BNF, RES. QB-201 (9)-FOL.

Whitelocke, Bulstrode. *Journal of the Swedish Embassy in the Years 1653 and 1654*, vol. 1, edited by Charles Morton and Henry Reeve. London: John Edward Taylor, 1855.

Workshop of Franz Hogenberg (inventor and engraver). *König Heinrich der dritt des namen*. Cologne: workshop of Franz Hogenberg (printer and editor), 1589; engraving – Munich: BSB, Res/4° Gall.g. 302f-1 Historia.

Wunderbärlicher Abschiedt/ vnd seltzamer Todt/ Henrici des dritten . . . . s. l. 1589 – Wolfenbüttel: HAB, T: 946.4 Helmst. (23).

Zeyttung Auß Franckreich . . . . Augsburg: Josias Wörli, 1589 – Jena: ThULB, 4 Gall.II,66 (2).

Zoppino, Niccolò. *Barʒoleta novamente composta de la mossa facta per venetiani contra alo ilustrissimo Signore Alphonso duca terʒo de Ferrara.* Ferrara c. 1509.

Secondary Literature

Ahnert, Ruth. 'Maps versus Networks.' In *News Networks in Early Modern Europe*, edited by Joad Raymond and Noah Moxham, 130–57. Library of the Written Word, vol. 47. Leiden: Brill, 2016.

Ahnert, Ruth, Sebastian E. Ahnert, Catherine Nicole Coleman, and Scott B. Weingart. *The Network Turn: Changing Perspectives in the Humanities.* 1st ed. Cambridge: Cambridge University Press, 2020. https://doi.org/10.1017/9781108866804.

Arblaster, Paul. 'Posts, Newsletters, Newspapers: England in a European System of Communications.' *Media History* 11, no. 1–2 (2005), 21–36. https://doi.org/10.1080/1368880052000342398.

Bauer, Oswald. *Pasquille in den Fuggerʒeitungen. Spott- und Schmähgedichte ʒwischen Polemik und Kritik (1568–1605).* Munich: Böhlau, 2008.

Beals, Melodee H. and Emily Bell, with contributions by Ryan Cordell, Paul Fyfe, Isabel Galina Russell, Tessa Hauswedell, Clemens Neudecker, Julianne Nyhan, Mila Oiva, Sebastian Padó, Miriam Peña Pimentel, Lara Rose, Hannu Salmi, Melissa Terras, and Lorella Viola. *The Atlas of Digitised Newspapers and Metadata: Reports from Oceanic Exchanges. Loughborough: 2020.* https://doi.org./10.6084/m9.figshare.11560059.

Behringer, Wolfgang. 'Communications Revolutions: A Historiographical Concept.' *German History* 24, no. 3 (1 August 2006), 333–74. https://doi.org/10.1191/0266355406gh378oa.

Bellingradt, Daniel. 'Annäherungen an eine Kommunikationsgeschichte der Frühen Neuzeit.' *Jahrbuch für Kommunikationsgeschichte* 20 (2018), 16–21.

Bellingradt, Daniel and Massimo Rospocher, eds. 'The Intermediality of Early Modern Communication.' Special issue, *Cheiron* 2 (2021).

Bellingradt, Daniel, Paul Nelles, and Jeroen Salman, eds. *Books in Motion in Early Modern Europe: Beyond Production, Circulation and Consumption.* London: Macmillan, 2017.

Boys, Jayne E. E. *London's News Press and the Thirty Years War.* Studies in Early Modern Cultural, Political and Social History, vol. 12. Woodbridge: Boydell Press, 2011.

Brandtzæg, Siv Gøril. '*Skillingsvisene i Norge 1550–1950: Historien om et forsømt forskningsfelt/*Broadside Ballads in Norway 1550–1950: The Story of an Overlooked Research Field.' *Edda* 105, no. 2 (2018), 93–109.

Braudel, Fernand. *The Mediterranean and the Mediterranean World in the Age of Philip II.* London: Collins, 1972.

Brayshay, Mark. *Land Travel and Communications in Tudor and Stuart England: Achieving a Joined-up Realm.* Liverpool: Liverpool University Press, 2014.

Brednich, Rolf Wilhelm. *Die Liedpublizistik im Flugblatt des 15. bis 17. Jahrhunderts*, 2 vols. Baden-Baden: Koerner, 1974–5.

Brownlees, Nicholas. *The Language of Periodical News in Seventeenth-Century England.* Newcastle upon Tyne: Cambridge Scholars Pub, 2011.

Bunout, Estelle, Maud Ehrmann, and Frédéric Clavert, eds. *Digitised Newspapers: A New Eldorado for Historians? Reflections on Tools, Methods and Epistemology.* Berlin: De Gruyter Oldenbourg, 2023. https://doi.org/10.1515/9783110729214.

Burke, Peter. 'Early Modern Venice as a Center of Information and Communication.' In *Venice Reconsidered: The History and Civilisation of an Italian City-State*, edited by John Jeffries Martin and Dennis Romano, 389–419. London: Johns Hopkins University Press, 2000.

Cassan, Michel. 'La guerre en discours. L'année 1589 en France.' In *Le bruit des armes. Mises en formes et désinformations en Europe pendant les guerres de Religion (1560–1610)*, edited by Jérémie Foa and Paul-Alexis Mellet, 259–75. Paris: Honoré Champion, 2012.

Castillo Gomez, Antonio. 'The Alborayque and Other Street Readings in the Early Modern Hispanic World.' In *Kreuʒ- und Querʒüge. Beiträge ʒu einer literarischen Anthropologie*, edited by Harm-Peer Zimmermann, Peter O. Büttner, and Bernhard Tschofen, 167–89. Hannover: Wehrhahn Verlag, 2019.

Colavizza, Giovanni, Mario Infelise, and Frédéric Kaplan. 'Mapping the Early Modern News Flow: An Enquiry by Robust Text Reuse Detection.' In *Social Informatics*. Lecture Notes in Computer Science, edited by Luca Maria Aiello and Daniel McFarland, 244–53. Cham: Springer International Publishing, 2015. https://doi.org/10.1007/978-3-319-15168-7_31.

Cordell, Ryan. 'Oceanic Exchanges.' http://oceanicexchanges.github.io/ (6 January 2023).

Cordell, Ryan. 'Viral Texts Project.' http://viraltexts.github.io/ (6 January 2023).

Cotton, Anthony N. B. 'John Dillingham, Journalist of the Middle Group.' *The English Historical Review* 93, no. 369 (1978), 817–34.

Dahl, Folke. *A Bibliography of English Corantos and Periodical Newsbooks 1620–1642*. Stockholm: Almquist och Wiksell, 1953.

Dahl, Folke. *Amsterdam Earliest Newspaper Centre of Western Europe: New Contributions to the History of the First Dutch and French Corantos*. Dordrecht: Springer Netherlands, 1939.

De Bolla, Peter. *The Architecture of Concepts: The Historical Formation of Human Rights*. New York: Fordham University Press, 2013.

De Bolla, Peter, Ewan Jones, Paul Nulty, Gabriel Recchia, and John Regan. 'Distributional Concept Analysis.' *Contributions to the History of Concepts* 14, no. 1 (2019), 66–92. https://doi.org/10.3167/choc.2019.140104.

De Vivo, Filippo. 'Microhistories of Long-Distance Information: Space, Movement and Agency in the Early Modern News.' *Past & Present* 242, Suppl. 14 (2019), 179–214. https://academic.oup.com/past/article/242/Supplement_14/179/5637705.

Degl'Innocenti, Luca and Massimo Rospocher, eds. 'Street Singers in Renaissance Europe.' Special issue, *Renaissance Studies* 33, no. 1 (2019).

Degl'Innocenti, Luca and Massimo Rospocher. 'Urban Voices: The Hybrid Figure of the Street Singer in Renaissance Italy.' *Renaissance Studies* 33, no. 1 (2019), 17–41.

Der Weduwen, Arthur. 'Competition, Choice and Diversity in the Newspaper Trade of the Dutch Golden Age.' *Early Modern Low Countries* 2 (2018), 7–23.

Der Weduwen, Arthur. *Dutch and Flemish Newspapers of the Seventeenth Century, 1618–1700*, 2 vols. Leiden: Brill, 2017.

DiCenzo, Maria. 'Remediating the Past: Doing "Periodical Studies" in the Digital Era.' *English Studies in Canada* 41, no. 1 (2015), 19–39. https://ojs.lib.uwo.ca/index.php/esc/article/view/9556.

Dooley, Brendan. 'International News Flows in the Seventeenth Century: Problems and Prospects.' In *News Networks in Early Modern Europe*, edited by Joad Raymond and Noah Moxham, 158–77. Library of the Written Word, vol. 47. Leiden: Brill, 2016.

Droste, Heiko. *The Business of News*. Leiden-Boston: Brill, 2021.

Dutch Song Database, www.liederenbank.nl/resultaatlijst.php?zoekveld=greensleeves&submit=search&enof=EN-zoeken&zoekop=allewoordenlied&sorteer=jaar&lan=en&wc=true (26 September 2022).

Frank, Joseph. *The Beginnings of the English Newspaper, 1620–1660*. Cambridge, MA: Harvard University Press, 1961.

Frearson, Michael. 'London Corantos in the 1620s.' *Studies in Newspaper and Periodical History* 1, no. 1–2 (1993), 3–17. https://doi.org/10.1080/13688809309357883.

Fyfe, Paul. 'An Archaeology of Victorian Newspapers.' *Victorian Periodicals Review* 49, no. 4 (2016), 546–77. https://doi.org/10.1353/vpr.2016.0039.

Gomis Coloma, Juan. *Menudencias de imprenta. Producción y circulación de la literatura popular (Valencia, siglo XVIII)*. Valencia: Institució Alfons el Magnànim, 2015.

Grijp, Louis P. *Het Nederlandse Lied in de Gouden Eeuw*. Amsterdam: Meertens Institute, 1991.

Haffemeyer, Stéphane. 'Public and Secret Networks of News: The Declaration of War of the Turks against the Empire in 1683.' In *News Networks in Early Modern Europe*, edited by Joad Raymond and Noah Moxham, 805–23. Leiden: Brill, 2016. https://doi.org/10.1163/9789004277199.

Hanson, Laurence. *English Newsbooks: 1620–1641*. London: Bibliographical Society, 1938.

Hellwig, Fritz. 'Einleitung.' In *Franz Hogenberg / Abraham Hogenberg: Franz Hogenberg – Abraham Hogenberg. Geschichtsblätter*, edited by Fritz Hellwig, 7–30. Nördlingen: Uhl, 1983.

Henry, Chrischinda. 'From Beggar to Virtuoso: The Street Singer in the Netherlandish Visual Tradition, 1500–1600.' *Renaissance Studies* 33, no. 1 (2018), 138–56.

Hyde, Jenni. 'From Page to People: Ballad Singers as Intermediaries in the Early Modern Graphosphere.' In *Transactions of XI International Conference on the History of Written Culture (CIHCE)*. Gijon: Trea, forthcoming.

Hyde, Jenni. *Singing the News: Ballads in Mid-Tudor England*. Abingdon: Routledge, 2018.

Iglesias Castellano, Abel. *Entre la voz y el texto: los ciegos oracioneros y papelistas en la España moderna (1500–1836)*. Madrid: Consejo superior de investigaciones, 2022.

Jones, Steven E. *Roberto Busa, S. J., and the Emergence of Humanities Computing: The Priest and the Punched Cards*. New York: Routledge, 2016.

Keck, Jana, Mila Oiva, and Paul Fyfe. 'Lajos Kossuth and the Transnational News: A Computational and Multilingual Approach to Digitized Newspaper Collections.' *Media History* (2022), 1–18. https://doi.org/10.1080/13688804.2022.2146905.

Kinsbruner, Jay. *Independence in Spanish America: Civil Wars, Revolutions, and Underdevelopment.* Albuquerque: University of New Mexico Press, 2000.

Kohlndorfer, Ruth. *Diplomatie und Gelehrtenrepublik. Die Kontakte des französischen Gesandten Jacques Bongars (1554–1612).* Tübingen: Max Niemeyer, 2009.

Kortti, Jukka, *Media in History: An Introduction to the Meanings and Transformations of Communication over Time.* London: Red Globe Press, 2019.

Koszyk, Kurt. *Deutsche Presse im 19. Jahrhundert. Geschichte der deutschen Presse.* Berlin: Colloquium Verlag, 1966.

Lahti, Leo, Niko Ilomäki, and Mikko Tolonen. 'A Quantitative Study of History in the English Short-Title Catalogue (ESTC), 1470–1800.' *LIBER Quarterly* 25, no. 2 (2015), 87–116. https://doi.org/10.18352/lq.10112.

Lahti, Leo, Jani Marjanen, Hege Roivainen, and Mikko Tolonen. 'Bibliographic Data Science and the History of the Book (c. 1500–1800).' *Cataloging & Classification Quarterly* 57, no. 1 (2019), 5–23. https://doi.org/10.1080/01639374.2018.1543747.

Lerma Mayer, Adán Israel, Adán Israel Lerma Mayer, Ximena Gutierrez-Vasques, Ernesto Priani Saiso, and Hannu Salmi. 'Underlying Sentiments in 1867: A Study of News Flows on the Execution of Emperor Maximilian I of Mexico in Digitized Newspaper Corpora.' *Digital Humanities Quarterly* 16, no. 4 (2022). https://www.digitalhumanities.org/dhq/vol/16/4/000649/000649.html

Lindemann, Margot. *Deutsche Presse bis 1815. Geschichte der deutschen Presse Teil I.* Berlin: Colloquium Verlag, 1969.

Lundell, Patrik, Hannu Salmi, Erik Edoff, Jani Marjanen, Heli Rantala, eds., *Information Flows across the Baltic Sea: Towards a Computational Approach to Media History.* Lund: Media History Archives, 2023. DOI:10.54292/s6au8axqht

Marsh, Christopher. '"Fortune My Foe": The Circulation of an English Super-Tune.' In *Identity, Intertextuality, and Performance in Early Modern Song Culture*, edited by Dieuwke van der Poel, Louis P. Grijp, and Wim van Anrooij, 308–30. Leiden: Brill, 2016.

Marsh, Christopher. 'A Woodcut and Its Wanderings in Seventeenth-Century England.' *Huntington Library Quarterly* 79, no. 2 (2016), 245–62.

Marsh, Christopher. *Music and Society in Early Modern England.* Oxford: Oxford University Press, 2012.

McAleer, John J. 'Ballads on the Spanish Armada.' *Texas Studies in English Literature and Language* 4 (1963), 602–12.

McIlvenna, Una. *Singing the News of Death: Execution Ballads in Europe, 1500–1900.* Oxford: Oxford University Press, 2022.

McIlvenna, Una. 'The Rich Merchant Man, or, What the Punishment of Greed Sounded Like in Early Modern English Ballads.' *Huntington Library Quarterly* 79, no. 2 (2016), 279–99.

McIlvenna, Una. 'When the News was Sung: Ballads as News Media in Early Modern Europe.' *Media History* 22, no. 3–4 (2016), 317–33.

McIlvenna, Una. 'The Power of Music: the Significance of Contrafactum in Execution Ballads.' *Past and Present* 229, no. 1 (2015), 47–89.

McShane, Angela. 'Typography Matters: Branding Ballads and Gelding Curates in Stuart England.' In *Book Trade Connections from the Seventeenth to the Twentieth Centuries*, edited by John Hinks and Catherine Armstrong, 19–44. London: British Library, 2008.

Miralles, Eulàlia. 'Versos efímeros para la guerra de Separación catalana.' *Bibliofília* 121, no. 2 (2019), 313–28.

Moisi, Stephanie. 'Das politische Lied der Reformationszeit (1517–1555). Ein Beitrag zur Kommunikationsgeschichte des Politischen im 16. Jahrhundert.' PhD diss., Graz, 2015.

Moureau, François. *Répertoire des nouvelles à la main. Dictionnaire de la presse manuscrite clandestine XVIe–XVIIIe siècle.* Oxford: Voltaire Foundation, 1999.

Muddiman, Joseph George. *A History of English Journalism: To the Foundation of The Gazette.* London: Longmans, 1908.

Mussell, James. 'Elemental Forms: The Newspaper as Popular Genre in the Nineteenth Century.' *Media History* 20, no. 1 (2014), 4–20. https://doi.org/10.1080/13688804.2014.880264.

Mussell, James. *The Nineteenth-Century Press in the Digital Age.* New York: Palgrave Macmillan, 2012.

Nicholson, Bob. 'The Digital Turn: Exploring the Methodological Possibilities of Digital Newspaper Archives.' *Media History* 19, no. 1 (2013), 59–73. https://doi.org/10.1080/13688804.2012.752963.

Oettinger, Rebecca. *Music as Propaganda in the German Reformation.* Aldershot: Ashgate, 2001.

Osterhammel, Jürgen. *The Transformation of the World: A Global History of the Nineteenth Century.* Princeton, NJ: Princeton University Press, 2014.

Pérez Fernández, José María and Edward Wilson-Lee. *Hernando Colón's New World of Books: Toward a Cartography of Knowledge.* New Haven: Yale University Press, 2021.

Pettegree, Andrew. *The Invention of News: How the World Came to Know About Itself.* New Haven: Yale University Press, 2014.

Phelps Brown, E. H. and Sheila V. Hopkins. 'Seven Centuries of Building Wages.' *Economica*, New Series 22, no. 87 (1955), 296–314.

Poe, Marshall T. *A History of Communications: Media and Society from the Evolution of Speech to the Internet*. Cambridge: Cambridge University Press, 2010.

Putnam, Lara. 'The Transnational and the Text-Searchable: Digitized Sources and the Shadows They Cast.' *The American Historical Review* 121, no. 2 (2016), 377–402. https://doi.org/10.1093/ahr/121.2.377.

Raymond, Joad. *The News in Europe*. London: Allen Lane, forthcoming.

Raymond, Joad. 'Books as Diplomatic Agents: Milton in Sweden.' In *Cultures of Diplomacy and Literary Writing in the Early Modern World: New Approaches*, edited by Tracey A. Sowerby and Joanna Craigwood, 131–45. Oxford: Oxford University Press, 2019.

Raymond, Joad. 'International News and the Seventeenth-Century English Newspaper.' In *Not Dead Things: The Dissemination of Popular Print in Britain, Italy, and the Low Countries, 1500–1900*, edited by Joad Raymond, Jeroen Salman, and Roeland Harms, 229–51. Leiden: Brill, 2013.

Raymond, Joad. 'Dillingham, John (Fl. 1639–1649), Journalist.' In *Oxford Dictionary of National Biography*. Oxford: Oxford University Press, 2004. https://www.oxforddnb.com/display/10.1093/ref:odnb/978019861 4128.001.0001/odnb-9780198614128-e-55915.

Raymond, Joad. *Pamphlets and Pamphleteering in Early Modern Britain*. Cambridge: Cambridge University Press, 2003.

Raymond, Joad. *The Invention of the Newspaper: English Newsbooks, 1641– 1649*. Oxford: Oxford University Press, 1996.

Raymond, Joad and Noah Moxham, eds. *News Networks in Early Modern Europe*. Leiden: Brill, 2016.

Rospocher, Massimo. 'News in Verse: The Battle of Polesella (1509) between Imagination, Communication, and Information.' In *Turning Tales: Essays on History and Literature in Honor of Guido Ruggiero*, edited by Mary Lindemann and Deanna Shemek. Newark: University of Delaware Press, forthcoming.

Rospocher, Massimo. '"In vituperium Status Veneti": The case of Niccolò Zoppino.' *The Italianist* 34, no. 3 (2014), 349–61.

Rospocher, Massimo, ed. *Beyond the Public Sphere: Opinions, Publics, Spaces in Early Modern Europe.* Berlin: Dunker & Humlot, 2012.

Rospocher, Massimo and Rosa Salzberg. *Il mercato dell'informazione. Notizie vere, false e sensazionali nella Venezia del Cinquecento.* Venice: Marsilio, 2022.

Rospocher, Massimo and Rosa Salzberg. 'An Evanescent Public Sphere: Voices, Spaces, and Publics in Venice During the Italian Wars.' In *Beyond the Public Sphere: Opinions, Publics, and Spaces in Early Modern Europe*, edited by Massimo Rospocher, 93–114. Berlin-Bologna: Dunker & Humlot-Il Mulino, 2012.

Salmi, Hannu. *What is Digital History?* Cambridge: Polity, 2021.

Salmi, Hannu, Asko Nivala, Heli Rantala, Reetta Sippola, Aleksi Vesanto, and Filip Ginter. 'Återanvändningen av text i den finska tidningspressen 1771–1853.' *Historisk tidskrift för Finland* 103, no. 1 (2018), 46–76.

Salmi, Hannu, Jukka Sarjala and Heli Rantala. 'Embryonic Modernity: Infectious Dynamics in Early Nineteenth-Century Finnish Culture.' *International Journal for History, Culture and Modernity* 8, no. 2 (2020), 105–27. https://doi.org/10.1163/22130624-00802001.

Salzberg, Rosa. *Ephemeral City: Cheap Print and Urban Culture in Renaissance Venice.* Manchester: Manchester University Press, 2014.

Salzberg, Rosa and Massimo Rospocher. 'Murder Ballads: Singing, Hearing, Writing and Reading about Murder in Renaissance Italy.' In *Murder in Renaissance Italy*, edited by Trevor Dean and Kate Lowe, 164–88. Cambridge: Cambridge University Press, 2017.

Salzberg, Rosa and Massimo Rospocher. 'Street Singers in Italian Renaissance Urban Culture and Communication.' *Cultural and Social History* 9, no. 1 (2012), 9–26.

Schäfer-Griebel, Alexandra. 'Writing an Integrated History of Mediated Communication for the "Period of the League". Or: How Henry III and

Royal Camp Initiated and Disseminated News Publications in 1589.' In 'The Intermediality of Early Modern Communication,' edited by Daniel Bellingradt and Massimo Rospocher. Special issue, *Cheiron* 2 (2021), 50–68.

Schäfer-Griebel, Alexandra. 'Die Arbeitspraxis im Nachrichtendruckgewerbe. Religionskriegsnachrichten im Heiligen Römischen Reich um 1590.' *Jahrbuch für Kommunikationsgeschichte* 20 (2018), 42–70.

Schäfer-Griebel, Alexandra. *Die Medialität der Französischen Religionskriege. Frankreich und das Heilige Römische Reich 1589.* Stuttgart: Steiner, 2018.

Schäfer-Griebel, Alexandra. 'Acquisition and Handling of News on the French Wars of Religion in Cologne. The Case of Hermann Weinsberg, with Particular Focus on the Engravings by Franz Hogenberg.' In *News Networks in Early Modern Europe*, edited by Joad Raymond and Noah Moxham, 695–715. Leiden: Brill, 2016.

Schäfer-Griebel, Alexandra. 'Les guerres de religion en France dans les gravures de Hogenberg.' In *Médialité et interprétation contemporaine des premières guerres de Religion*, edited by Lothar Schilling and Gabriele Haug-Moritz, 98–120. Berlin: De Gruyter, 2014.

Schobesberger, Nikolaus. 'Mapping the Fuggerzeitungen: The Geographical Issues of an Information Network.' In *News Networks in Early Modern Europe*, edited by Joad Raymond and Noah Moxham, 216–40. Leiden: Brill, 2016. https://doi.org/10.1163/9789004277199.

Slauter, Will. 'Le paragraphe mobile: circulation et transformation des informations dans le monde atlantique du 18e siècle.' *Annales: Histoire, Sciences Sociales* 67, no. 2 (2012), 253–78.

Slauter, Will. 'The Paragraph as Information Technology: How News Travelled in the Eighteenth-Century Atlantic World.' *Annales: Histoire, Sciences Sociales* 67, no. 2 (2012), 363–89.

Soll, Jacob. *The Information Master: Jean-Baptiste Colbert's Secret State Intelligence System.* Ann Arbor: University of Michigan Press, 2009.

Stöber, Rudolf. *Deutsche Pressegeschichte: Von den Anfängen bis zur Gegenwart*. 3rd ed. Köln: Herbert von Halem Verlag, 2014.

Taylor, Andrew. *The Songs and Travels of a Tudor Minstrel: Richard Sheale of Tamworth*. York: York Medieval Press, 2012.

Thompson, William Forde. *Music, Thought and Feeling: Understanding the Psychology of Music*. Oxford: Oxford University Press, 2009.

Tommila, Päiviö. 'Yhdestä lehdestä sanomalehdistöksi 1809–1859 (From one newspaper into a press, 1809–1859, in Finnish).' In *Suomen lehdistön historia. Sanomalehdistön vaiheet vuoteen 1905*, edited by Päiviö Tommila, 77–265. Kuopio: Kustannuskiila, 1988.

Van der Poel, Dieuwke. 'Exploring Love's Options: Song and Youth Culture in the Sixteenth Century Netherlands.' In *Identity, Intertextuality, and Performance in Early Modern Song Culture*, edited by Dieuwke van der Poel, Louis P. Grijp, and Wim van Anrooij, 209–39. Leiden: Brill, 2016.

Van Groesen, Michiel. *Amsterdam's Atlantic: Print Culture and the Making of Dutch Brazil*. Philadelphia: University of Pennsylvania Press, 2017.

Van Orden, Kate. 'Cheap Print and Street Song following the Saint Bartholomew's Massacres of 1572.' In *Music and the Cultures of Print*, edited by Kate van Orden, 271–323. Abingdon: Routledge, 2017.

Verheul, Jaap, Hannu Salmi, Martin Riedl, Asko Nivala, Lorella Viola, Jana Keck, and Emily Bell. 'Using Word Vector Models to Trace Conceptual Change over Time and Space in Historical Newspapers, 1840–1914.' *Digital Humanities Quarterly* 16, no. 2 (2022). https://www.digitalhumanities.org/dhq/vol/16/2/000550/000550.html

Watt, Tessa. *Cheap Print and Popular Piety, 1550–1640*. Cambridge: Cambridge University Press, 1991.

Williams, Sarah. *Damnable Practises: Witches, Dangerous Women, and Music in Seventeenth-Century English Broadside Ballads*. Farnham: Ashgate, 2015.

Wilson, Blake. 'The *Cantastorie/Canterino/Cantimbanco* as Musician.' *Italian Studies* 71, no. 2 (2016), 154–70.

Wilson-Lee, Edward. 'The Bull and the Moon: Broadside Ballads and the Public Sphere at the Time of the Northern Rising (1569–70).' *Review of English Studies* 63, no. 259 (2012), 225–42.

Wiltenberg, Joy. 'Ballads and the Emotional Life of Crime.' In *Ballads and Broadsides in Britain, 1500–1800*, edited by Patricia Fumerton, Anita Guerrini, and Kris McAbee, 173–86. Farnham: Ashgate, 2010.

Wiltenburg, Joy. 'True Crime: The Origins of Modern Sensationalism.' *American Historical Review* 109, no. 5 (2004), 1379–80.

Zwierlein, Cornel A. *Discorso und Lex Dei. Die Entstehung neuer Denkrahmen im 16. Jahrhundert und die Wahrnehmung der französischen Religionskriege in Italien und Deutschland*. Göttingen: Vandenhoeck & Ruprecht, 2006.

Zwierlein, Cornel A. 'Komparative Kommunikationsgeschichte und Kulturtransfer im 16. Jahrhundert. Methodische Überlegungen entwickelt am Beispiel der Kommunikation über die französischen Religionskriege (1559–1598) in Deutschland und Italien.' In *Kulturtransfer. Kulturelle Praxis im 16. Jahrhundert*, edited by Wolfgang Schmale, 85–120. Innsbruck: De Gruyter, 2003.

Cambridge Elements ⌖

Publishing and Book Culture

SERIES EDITOR
Samantha Rayner
University College London

Samantha Rayner is Professor of Publishing and Book Cultures at UCL.She is also Director of UCL's Centre for Publishing, co-Director of the Bloomsbury CHAPTER (Communication History, Authorship, Publishing, Textual Editing and Reading) and co-Chair of the Bookselling Research Network.

ASSOCIATE EDITOR
Leah Tether
University of Bristol

Leah Tether is Professor of Medieval Literature and Publishing at the University of Bristol. With an academic background in medieval French and English literature and a professional background in trade publishing, Leah has combined her expertise and developed an international research profile in book and publishing history from manuscript to digital.

About the Series

This series aims to fill the demand for easily accessible, quality texts available for teaching and research in the diverse and dynamic fields of Publishing and Book Culture. Rigorously researched and peer-reviewed Elements will be published under themes, or 'Gatherings'. These Elements should be the first check point for researchers or students working on that area of publishing and book trade history and practice: we hope that, situated so logically at Cambridge University Press, where academic publishing in the UK began, it will develop to create an unrivalled space where these histories and practices can be investigated and preserved.

Cambridge Elements ☰

Publishing and Book Culture

Publishing and Book History

Gathering Editor: Andrew Nash

Andrew Nash is Reader in Book History and Director of the London Rare Books School at the Institute of English Studies, University of London. He has written books on Scottish and Victorian Literature, and edited or co-edited numerous volumes including, most recently, *The Cambridge History of the Book in Britain, Volume 7* (Cambridge University Press, 2019).

Gathering Editor: Leah Tether

Leah Tether is Professor of Medieval Literature and Publishing at the University of Bristol. With an academic background in medieval French and English literature and a professional background in trade publishing, Leah has combined her expertise and developed an international research profile in book and publishing history from manuscript to digital.

Elements in the Gathering

Publication and the Papacy in Late Antique and Medieval Europe
Samu Niskanen

Publishing in Wales: Renaissance and Resistance
Jacob D. Rawlins

The People of Print: Seventeenth-Century England
Rachel Stenner, Kaley Kramer and Adam James Smith *et al.*

Printed in the United States
by Baker & Taylor Publisher Services